The

# Single

# Father's

# Guide
## To Life, Cooking and Baseball

For Nikki Lockridge

# The
# Single

# Father's

# Guide
## To Life, Cooking and Baseball

## BY MATTHEW S. FIELD

Arundel Publishing
PO Box 377
Warwick, NY 10990

www.arundelpublishing.com

www.thesinglefathersguide.com

## OTHER BOOKS BY MATTHEW S. FIELD

### Illustrated Children's Literature

*Father Like a Tree*
*The Three Pigs, Business School, and Wolfe Hash Stew*

### Mainstream Fiction

*The Dream Seeker*

# CONTENTS

# PROLOGUE
## IT'S A GAME OF INCHES

Single fatherhood? Very likely, you did *not* plan to be here. Whether you said, "I do," or "I do *tonight*," you probably hadn't considered the possibility that you wouldn't have a partner to help raise your child or children. Divorced? Widower? A little surprise? Okay, perhaps a few single fathers actually planned to be a single father, and that's cool, too.

"The number of men who list themselves as single fathers has increased dramatically in the past 20 years.[1]" According to the U.S. Census Bureau, there were 1.8 million single fathers in the United States in 2010. Of that number, approximately 46 percent were divorced, 30 percent were never married, 19 percent were separated, and 6 percent were widowers. Among those, about 154,000 were stay-at-home dads.[2]

*Life will always throw you curves, just keep fouling them off . . .*
*the right pitch will come, but when it does,*
*be prepared to run the bases.*
**—Rick Maksian**

Regardless of the path, you're in good company. Counted among the ranks of current and former single fathers are musician/activist Bob Geldof, baseball slugger Mark McGuire, actor Al Pacino, basketball star Dwyane Wade, actor Colin Farrell, international soccer great Cristiano Ronaldo, musician Lenny Kravitz, and, ahem, me.

You may know how to change your oil and flush the coolant in your car. Maybe you're the best defense attorney in the city or a high-powered captain of industry. You might be able to fillet a trout or field dress a deer. You may even know the answer to the question, "Who played third base for the '42 St. Louis Browns?" or recite the infield fly rule verbatim. Regardless of who you are, what you know, or the specifics of your situation, it's time to add another dimension to your toolbox. It's time to put up because someone, or maybe more than one someone, depends on you part of the time or all of the time. Let's go, Dad. You need to step up to the plate.

As far back as I can remember, I have heard parents lament (particularly when their kids are creating havoc), "Well, children don't come with a user's manual." If a user's manual doesn't exist for families in which the mother and father share the responsibilities of making a home, earning a living, and raising the kids, there certainly is no step-by-step guide for the single father.

I wouldn't have ever considered a playbook for single fathers had I not, quite reluctantly, become a single father myself under circumstances worthy of a made-for-television movie.

On an unseasonably warm, early spring day in Saratoga Springs, New York, where I lived with my wife, Lori, and our two daughters, I clearly remember thinking to myself, "You know, you've got it pretty good."

At that time, I was a thirty-six-year-old middle manager working for a publicly traded company. Although I was a bit of a "road warrior," I was usually home on Mondays and Fridays, and my office was 3.2 miles from my front door, which allowed me to effectively balance my work with my family. I had two beautiful daughters, ages five and two. I married the girl with whom I'd fallen in love at first sight when I was a high school freshman. I wasn't able to convince her to date me until I was a junior in college, but eventually, she relented. Lori and I dated for six years before we married.

The two of us made a pretty good team. Whenever there was an opportunity for career advancement that came with the attached string of relocation, I was on the job at the new office the next business day while Lori coordinated moving our belongings with a company-provided relocation consultant. At each new home, we divided the labor: she took care of the inside of the house, while I maintained the outside. The two of us explored our new communities while we enjoyed five years together before our kids came along.

In 1997, while living in Rhode Island, we welcomed a baby girl at Women & Infants Hospital in Providence. A few years later, our second daughter was born in Stafford Springs, Connecticut. In 2003, the four of us enjoyed a life that included a nice home in a great, historic town where, after a three-hour car ride, we could have been in Montreal, Boston, or New York, or at one of the Great Lakes. We had health. We had love. We had, well, just about anything a person could want or need in life. Then, it seemed almost overnight, our lives turned from a fairytale into a tragedy.

I really do recall thinking to myself on that March afternoon as I drove back to my office after having lunch with my wife at home, "You know, you've got it pretty good. We aren't *there* yet, but for the first time in our lives, we can actually see where *there* is." Although, in truth, my very next thought was, "Every time you get things working in one place, you're asked to move to a new office." That night, I told Lori about my premonition.

Cue Coldplay's, "Viva La Vida."

We closed on our new home in September 2003. The picturesque Warwick Valley in New York is nestled among the foothills of the Catskills, the Taconics, and the Poconos in Orange County. The Town of Warwick is composed of several villages, including the town's namesake, Warwick, in addition to the Villages of Florida, Pine Island, and Greenwood Lake, where Babe Ruth amused himself during home stands and the off-season several decades earlier. Agriculture, in the form of apple orchards and onion fields, and an eclectic combination of artists, writers, and small-business owners, comprise its backdrop. Strange, considering the wonderful ambiance of the area and all the moves we'd made, but this was the first time that I felt uneasy when we relocated. It would turn out, I had good reason.

13

In October, Lori and I learned we'd welcome another child, a son, to our family. A couple of months later, my employer announced that it had acquired a competitor and would undergo an organizational restructuring. Considering I'd just relocated and had a consistent record of improving customer satisfaction and the company's bottom line I was confident that my job would not be affected. For Christmas, we gave ourselves a couple of "family" gifts, like a trip to Disney World in April before our son would be born in July. When we returned from our trip, we planned to get a German shepherd puppy.

On February 27, 2004, I was called to my employer's headquarters office in central New Jersey and informed that my job had been eliminated. Of course, I was disappointed, but a much bigger concern loomed. A few weeks later, Lori noticed a swelling at the base of her neck and left shoulder. Several doctors and specialists, starting with her primary care physician and ending with an infectious disease specialist, examined the inflammation during the next several days, but none were able to diagnose the condition. Finally, her doctor ordered a sonogram and determined a clot had partially blocked a blood vessel. Because the clot could have potentially broken loose and caused an aneurysm, Lori was admitted to the hospital and prescribed blood thinners to safely break down the clot.

While the mystery of the swelling had been solved, the question of what caused the clot still needed an answer. A day or two later and less than a week before the family was supposed to get on a plane to Orlando, I sat on an extremely uncomfortable chair and Lori lay in bed at St. Anthony's Community Hospital while her doctor confirmed the diagnosis: occult metastatic breast cancer. We canceled the trip and postponed the puppy.

*Adversity causes some men to break; others to break records.*
—**William Arthur Ward**

The lymph nodes under Lori's left arm had mounted a defense against the invading bad cells, creating a flood of white blood cells, which thickened her blood and clotted near the suspected primary cancer site. The treatment dissolved the clot, but the horse had escaped before the barn door was closed. Six months pregnant with our son, Lori immediately began chemotherapy treatments. In June, as I sat by her hospital bed, Lori gave birth to our son. Eight weeks later, blood tests detected no cancer. In October, however, the disease had returned with a vengeance. The cancer had metastasized first to her spinal fluid, then to her liver. Fewer than eight months after having our son and ten months after she was first diagnosed, Lori passed away in the hospital as I sat there holding her hand. It had been less than two years since I commented to myself about our perfect life, "You know, you've got it pretty good."

If there is one thing I've learned about a good made-for-television movie, it is that the protagonist, after facing a difficult or painful setback, somehow dusts himself off and steps back into the box.

Since February 4, 2005, I have been a single father of two daughters and a son, who were seven years old, five years old, and seven months old, respectively, when they lost their mother. And, no, there weren't any instructions. No single father's manual to guide someone like me as I began to deal with the emotional and physical needs that my children and I have experienced as I raise them without a mother.

> *When the going gets weird,*
> *the weird turn pro.*
> —Hunter S. Thompson

Forging ahead, in the context of an entirely new framework for our lives, I reverted to the lessons I'd learned to guide me, although I may not have been so appreciative at the time. I recalled everything from the Red Cross babysitting course my mother insisted I complete when I was ten years old to my summer job as a short-order cook at my uncle's restaurant in Florissant, Missouri, to the idea of the "balanced man," espoused by my college fraternity. I even applied some of the lessons gleaned from the scores of leadership classes I attended during nearly two decades of climbing the corporate ladder. Mostly, though, I relied on two fundamental ideas, which are often considered clichés. First, the lesson that I had so personally re-learned: "If you have your health, you have everything." The second: "Baseball is a metaphor for life."

When I'd heard people say, "If you have your health, you have everything," I thought I got it—but I only understood the words, not the devastating effects of a terminal illness on a loved one. Lori's illness and death really drove home the point. So, my first priority would be to keep my family healthy. Again, from my own experience, diet, exercise, and rest were the variables in the health equation that I could most easily control.

Ever since I was a boy, I played organized and pick-up sports. My favorite had always been baseball, but at different times, I'd played basketball, football, and soccer. I didn't really understand the reasons my father and others said, "Baseball is a metaphor for life," unless he meant to imply that life was a game. As I played and then studied the game, I eventually "got" it.

*Baseball is an allegorical play about America, a poetic, complex, and subtle play of courage, fear, good luck, mistakes, patience about fate, and sober self-esteem.*

**—Saul Steinberg**

The baseball season is long, but doesn't last forever. Life sometimes seems long, but it, too, does not last forever. For an individual to be successful, he has to perform as an individual, like he does when he's at bat; but he also has to work as part of a team, like he does when he plays the field. In life, a person who has character and integrity must take responsibility for his own actions, as well as live and work in a series of communities to accomplish greater goals for the larger society. Finally, as Branch Rickey suggested, "Baseball is a game of inches," in which small changes, small improvements, applied consistently and every day, will make a big impact both for the individual and for the team in the long run. Like Kevin Costner's character, Crash Davis, lamented in the 1988 film *Bull Durham*:

> You know what the difference is between hitting .250 and hitting .300? I got it figured out. Twenty-five hits a year in 500 at bats is 50 points. Okay? There's 6 months in a season, that's about 25 weeks—you get one extra flare a week—just one—a gork, a ground ball with eyes, a dying quail—just one more dying quail a week and you're in Yankee Stadium![3]

In life, like in baseball, small improvements mean a lot. Bread is a simple and practical example of that idea. Okay, I know most of us grew up eating good old, all-American white bread. For many, old habits may be difficult to break, but check this out. A quick grocery store comparison of one particular brand indicates that a slice of wheat bread has ten fewer calories than the same brand's white bread; the wheat bread also has three grams more of dietary fiber compared to the white.

Assume you pack your grade-schooler's lunch every day. The little scholar usually finds in the lunch box a ham and cheese sandwich on white bread. Doing the math, the ten additional calories in the white than in the wheat, multiplied by two slices of bread each school day, multiplied by 180 days in the school year yields a grand total of 3,600 additional calories each school year! Considering the average child between the ages of four and eight requires between 1,400 and 2,000 calories per day[4], white bread sandwiches compared to wheat bread sandwiches add about two days worth of eating. Of course, wheat bread also contains three times the dietary fiber, keeps your child feeling fuller longer. Considering the "prevalence of obesity among children aged 6 to 11 years increased from 6.5% in 1980 to 19.6% in 2008[5]," saving twenty calories each day by switching your sandwich bread is an easy way to get ahead of the game.

So, single fathers, regardless of your situation, this book can be your user's manual. Whether you are divorced and share visitation rights with your ex-wife, or you're a young widower who has kids at home full-time, or you have some other permutation of a single father existence, these are your basic instructions. First, however, there are a few disclaimers.

Yes, this is a cookbook. I believe keeping your children healthy keeps your children happy, and keeping your children happy keeps you happy. I've included recipes and ideas for breakfast, lunch, dinner, and snacks. And depending on your perspective, don't worry that the recipes are too difficult or too gourmet for you to handle. I am no gourmet.

I'm also not a nutritionist. While I'm aware of calories, I don't count them. Moreover, I believe that nutrition is both a science and an art. Scientifically, our bodies need vitamins, minerals, proteins, carbohydrates, and fats to function properly. Artistically, there is more than one way to skin a . . . chicken breast. In this context, some nutritionists who read *The Single Father's Guide* will be critical of the fact that I prefer to use soy milk, artificial sweetener, or wheat flour in some of my recipes. Other nutritionists would have been critical that I use too much dairy, too much sugar, or not enough high-fiber foods. In the simplest terms, though, these are the recipes that I have used to keep my family healthy and able to enjoy active and fulfilling lives.

Finally, some of my suggestions and anecdotes come from my experience as a husband in a marriage that was a positive and rewarding experience. In the universe of single fathers, I realize that many readers are much more likely to be recently divorced. When there are no children involved, divorce is usually a moderately complicated breakup. When kids are involved, divorce is at best, civil, and at worst, ugly and painful. In the descriptions of my marriage, I in no way intend to insinuate that one circumstance of single fatherhood is more or less preferable. Regardless of the path that a man has taken to arrive at single fatherhood, we're all on the same road now.

*These are my new shoes. They're good shoes. They won't make you rich like me, they won't make you rebound like me, they definitely won't make you handsome like me. They'll only make you have shoes like me. That's it.*
—Charles Barkley

No, this is probably a life you didn't expect. Likely, it's a life you would have done just about anything to avoid. But, now, it's your life. You're a single father. Because you love your children, you'll do the best you can for them. Again, because you love your children, you'll do the best you can for *you*, too.

When you've finished reading, I hope you'll find *The Single Father's Guide* to be a recipe for creating a healthy, productive, and contented life for you and your family. Remember, it's a game of inches.

# LEADING OFF
## BREAKFAST

I know the metaphor has become a cliché, but I'll use it anyway.

If you've sat on an airplane and listened to the flight attendant monotonously spew the preflight safety instructions, at one point during the monologue, she says something like, "Should the plane experience a sudden drop in cabin pressure, oxygen masks will drop from the panel above your seat. Please put on your oxygen mask before you put on the masks of any children who may be traveling with you." Obviously, it is important to put on your mask first because if you pass out from a lack of oxygen, you can't help your children traveling with you, and, more likely than not, your children will not be able to help you.

In 1966, Chicago Bears running back Gale Sayers wrote his autobiography *I Am Third*[6]. As the title suggested, in Gale's own life, he was third, behind his God, who was first, and the people close to him, who were second. I believe, however, Gale Sayers' equation for his own life will not work for single dads.

Here's the thing: an adult man has needs. His basic needs include food, shelter, and clothing, progressing to intermediate needs like exercise, socialization, and purpose, and culminating in higher needs like love, beauty, and a desire to leave a legacy. The fact is that if a single father is not healthy and happy, he will find it a struggle to create a life and home in which his children can be healthy and happy.

So, this is The Single Father's Golden Rule #1: *Put on your oxygen mask first!*

# GOLDEN RULE #1:

*Put on your oxygen mask first!*

## Oatmeal à la Dad

2 cups water

1 cup milk

1½ cups old fashioned oatmeal

1 cup diced apple, with the
 skin left on

¼ cup raisins

1 tablespoon butter

1 dash salt

1 pinch cinnamon

1 pinch brown sugar

In a saucepan, bring the water, milk, salt, and butter to a boil. Reduce the heat to low-medium and add the diced apple, raisins, and oatmeal. Stir until thick. To serve, divide the oatmeal into individual bowls, and add a pinch of cinnamon and brown sugar to each. The preparation time is only 5 to 10 minutes, and feeds a single father and his three children.

I've completely stopped buying cold cereals, because I believe they generally have too much processed sugar. Even cereals that do not add much (or any) sugar are still what I refer to as "easy carbs"—carbohydrate-rich foods that are too easy to eat as a snack at two o'clock in the afternoon or two o'clock in the morning. So, I just stopped buying the stuff.

With hot cereals like oatmeal and cream of wheat, I can control the amount and the type of sugar in each serving. Like me, you've probably heard both sides of the debate concerning corn sugar (corn syrup) and processed cane sugar (white sugar). I work from the assumption that anything is all right if used in moderation, but I'll typically use brown sugar, honey, or artificial sweetener before I use white sugar. Moreover, even though hot cereal doesn't take long to prepare, it takes longer to make than it does to open a box, dump some flakes in a bowl, and pour milk over it. The extra time provides just enough of a pause to feel good and more in control of the choice I've made.

*Most ball games are lost, not won.*
—Casey Stengel

Here's another important principle on which I base my meal planning, which happens to be The Single Father's Golden Rule #2: *Include at least one vegetable or fruit with every meal.* It doesn't have to be fancy or complicated. Slice an apple. Peel an orange. Put a box of frozen vegetables in the microwave. In just about every case, even frozen or canned fruits or vegetables are better than nothing!

## GOLDEN RULE #2:
### *Include at least one vegetable or fruit with every meal.*

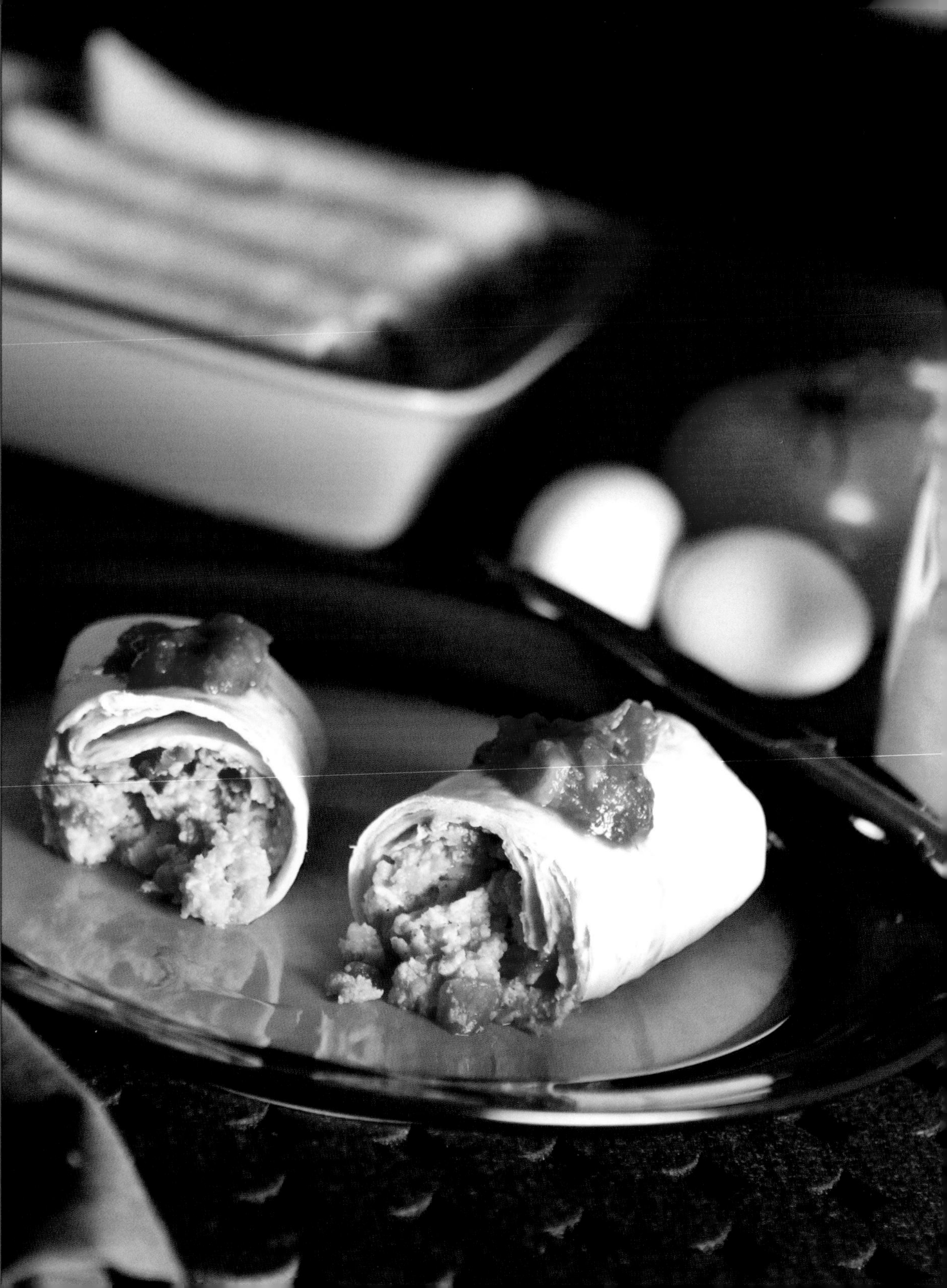

# Huevos Rancheros de Papi

6 eggs

1 cup shredded cheddar cheese

2 tablespoons vegetable oil

1 pinch black pepper

¾ cup diced tomato and onion
  or salsa

4 to 5 flour tortillas

Combine eggs, 1 tablespoon of vegetable oil, black pepper, and cheddar cheese in a mixing bowl. (Don't add salt! The cheddar cheese has plenty of sodium, which I've learned the hard way!) Beat with a fork until ingredients combine. Pour 1 tablespoon of vegetable oil onto the frying pan so the cooking surface is completely covered. Add ingredients, cook over medium-high heat, and stir gently with a spatula until eggs are cooked. Place a portion of the cooked eggs on a flour tortilla, and add a heaping tablespoon of diced tomatoes and onions or salsa. Fold tortilla burrito-style or taco-style, and repeat until all eggs are used. The preparation time is 10 to 15 minutes, and feeds *uno papi* and his *tres muchachitos*.

No matter the circumstances that propelled you to single fatherhood, the process probably has been difficult for you, but it has likely been even more difficult for your children. If you are separated or divorced, each of your kids probably worry that he or she was part of the reason mom and dad aren't together. If you've lost your wife to an illness or an accident, the trauma of the loss is overwhelming for everyone, but you're the adult. You may be devastated, but at least you have a little life experience and perspective. The reality of losing a parent, a mother, truly changes a child's entire life paradigm. Why do you think some of the best-known fairy tales like *Snow White* and *Cinderella* begin with a premise that a little girl's mother has died? The answer is that it's just about the worst thing of which a child can conceive.

The first thing you need to do, Dad, is provide a safe environment in which your children can process their emotions. The first step to providing that environment is creating and maintaining a routine. There is comfort in familiarity. Adhering to a routine which your children already know is a demonstrable signal that, although life may never be the same, life with Daddy will be all right.

*My motto was always to keep swinging. Whether I was in a slump or feeling badly or having trouble off the field, the only thing to do was keep swinging.*
—**Hank Aaron**

The age of your children and the activities in which your children are involved will go a long way in determining your routine. If you work outside the home, then some changes to the old routine may be necessary. For example, while the children's mother used to be the person who dressed and fed the kids, now a "father's helper," a neighbor or a nanny, may take on that responsibility. If the children's mother waited at the bus stop when the kids got off the bus, now a day care provider may assume that responsibility. If you're fortunate enough to work from home, you can have a great deal more control and an ability to maintain the kids' routine. In any case, while some things may have to change, there is still a great deal of your family's activities that can continue and provide the tangible experience of a comforting routine.

If your daughter participated in Girl Scouts after school on Tuesdays, then make the effort to ensure she continues to participate in Girl Scouts on Tuesdays. If your son had basketball practice after school, make arrangements for him to continue to attend basketball practice after school. And, more personally, if your family always watched a pay-per-view movie, made popcorn, and sat on the floor with pillows and blankets every Friday for "family movie night," then, without question, continue to have family movie night!

I understand: continuing a family routine is easier said than done. However, "children need even more rest because grieving the changes in their lives takes a lot of energy," according to Kim Sumner-Mayer, a marriage and family therapist. "It is very common for children to be more susceptible to illness during the first year after a major loss; the stress affects their immune function, underscoring again the need for excellent nutrition and ample sleep."[7]

There will be many things that are outside your control, ranging from how your children interact at school with their peers in the context of their new situation at home, to the way your family and friends react to you after a divorce or the loss of your spouse. In the meantime, focus on the items you can control:

- Be consistent about bedtime and wake-up times. Kids' little bodies need proper rest, and getting consistent sleep will help them *feel* right.

- Maintain a consistent bedtime habit such as bath/shower times, brushing teeth, tuck-in, and reading a story.

- Encourage your children to continue their extracurricular activities, most of which are physically and intellectually beneficial and provide a natural, ad hoc support group.

- Continue your family traditions, which may include having dinner as a family, family movie night, going to breakfast at your favorite restaurant after church or synagogue, or driving to your favorite aunt's house for Thanksgiving dinner.

## GOLDEN RULE #3:

### *Maintain your routines and traditions.*

While the routine will provide a structure and an environment where your children can enjoy a sense of security, the regularity in the household activities will do the same for you, as the single dad, and much more. The constancy of your efforts will provide you with a peace of mind that you've done everything you've needed to do for your children, and you will also be in a position to more clearly see how you can better manage your time for some of your higher needs. It follows, then, that The Single Father's Golden Rule #3 is: *Maintain your routines and traditions.*

# Strawberry-Mango-Banana Smoothie to Go

3 cups milk

2 peeled bananas

1 cup frozen mango

1 cup frozen strawberries

1 cup raw or roasted cashews

1 heaping tablespoon of honey

Pour milk into blender. Add bananas, frozen mango, frozen strawberries, cashews, and honey. Blend. (You can substitute soy, almond, or coconut milk for cow's milk; and a tablespoon or two of protein powder, chia seeds, or flax seeds for cashews, based on personal preference.) The preparation time is about 2 minutes, and provides a light and healthy breakfast for one dad and three children who've overslept and need to be someplace 10 minutes ago.

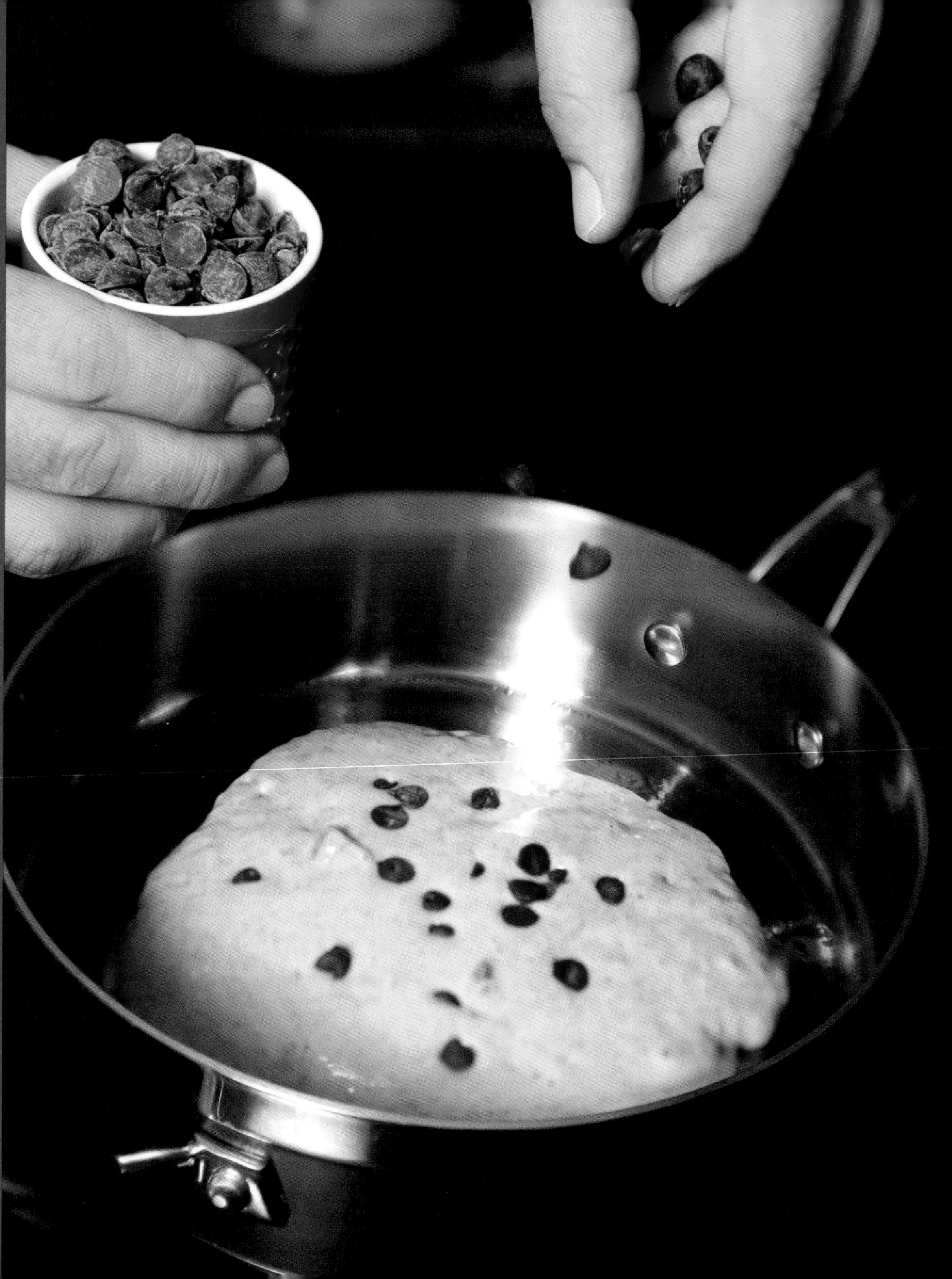

A banana was my mother's home remedy for a muscle cramp or charley horse when I was a kid. Potassium in bananas is great for active children (and dad). But, during the cold and flu season, you can swap a peeled and seeded orange for a banana to get a smoothie with an extra-healthy boost of vitamin C.

Whether you buy it prepackaged or buy or harvest it fresh and freeze it, frozen fruit is a versatile resource—and an exotic treat when certain fruits are out of season. Blackberries, blueberries, cherries, mangos, peaches, pineapple, raspberries, and strawberries all freeze well, making them a welcome addition to any smoothie, as well as being great in pancakes, waffles, and muffins. And this is an easy way to ensure a serving of fruits is part of your meal.

# Daddy's Chocolate Chip and Strawberry Cookie Pancakes

1⅔ cups whole wheat flour
⅓ cup soy flour
½ cup finely chopped walnuts
½ cup sugar substitute
½ cup chocolate chips
1 to 1½ cups fresh or thawed frozen strawberries, diced

1 teaspoon salt
1 tablespoon baking powder
2 ½ cups milk
2 to 3 eggs
2 tablespoons vegetable oil or melted butter

Combine whole wheat flour, soy flour, walnuts, sugar substitute, salt, and baking powder in a bowl and mix thoroughly. In a separate bowl, combine milk, eggs, and 1 tablespoon of vegetable oil or melted butter. Mix gently, and pour the wet ingredients into the bowl containing dry ingredients. Mix thoroughly, and stir in the chocolate chips and strawberries. Coat a well-heated pan (using medium to medium-high heat depending on your cooktop) with 1 tablespoon of vegetable oil or melted butter. Pour or ladle batter onto pan. Flip when the pancake is bubbling well. The preparation time is 20 to 25 minutes, makes approximately eight large pancakes, and feeds three very hungry children and their single dad on any Sunday morning.

In spite of the name, Daddy's Chocolate Chip and Strawberry Cookie Pancakes are significantly healthier, more substantial, and lower in calories than just about anything you'd find on your grocery store's shelves! And these pancakes are a perfect example of the premise "it's a game of inches."

First, the whole wheat flour in the recipe replaces the white flour in most premixed pancake batter with a substitute that is both high in fiber and more filling. Nutritionally, the whole wheat flour reduces about ten calories and two carbohydrates per pancake, but increases the protein content by almost a gram and dietary fiber by more than two grams.[8] In addition, a small amount of the flour is replaced with high-protein soy flour, which contains about 120 calories, just ten grams of carbohydrates, and almost ten grams of protein,[9] compared to the white flour, which contains 25 percent more calories, three times the carbohydrates, and only half of the protein.[10] That small modification will go unnoticed by even the most sensitive palate. The same is true for the finely chopped walnuts, which contribute to the "cookie" texture, but effectively takes the place of the grain flour and substitutes another high-protein, high-fiber, and mineral-laden food.

I understand that there are two camps when it comes to artificial sweeteners versus processed sugar. Folks who don't like artificial sweeteners may be concerned about its effects on the liver and its potential link to some illnesses. On the other hand, processed cane sugar is the simplest of simple

carbohydrates, has very little nutritional value, and, in large enough quantities, may contribute to childhood obesity, diabetes, and other ailments. There are almost 390 calories and 100 grams of carbohydrates in a half cup of sugar,[11] which translates to approximately 49 calories and 12.5 carbohydrate grams for the sugar in each conventional pancake.

Alternatives to both sugar and artificial sweeteners include xylitol and stevia extract, which have become more popular recently. Neither contributes to blood sugar spikes, and both are naturally derived, which are definite benefits. On the other hand, both are generally more expensive to buy than either sugar or artificial sweeteners.

Daddy's Chocolate Chip and Strawberry Cookie Pancakes is the single father's metaphorical "pitcher's best friend" when it comes to family meal planning. Not only do the pancakes provide a fun, tasty, well-balanced

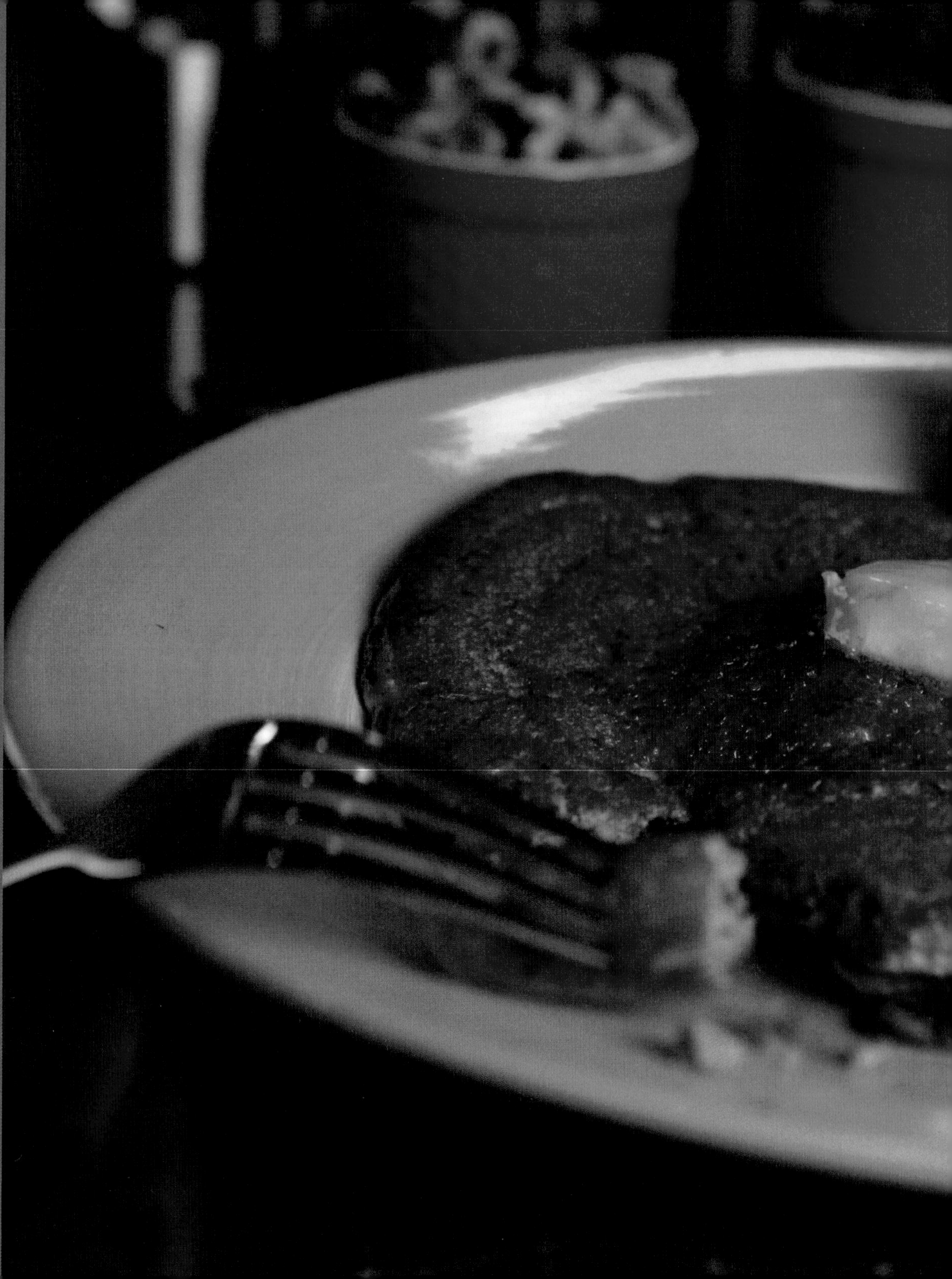

meal that includes protein in the form of soy flour, milk, and walnuts, along with high-fiber complex carbohydrates from whole wheat flour, but they are also filling. The strawberries comply with my rule to include a fruit or vegetable at every meal and provide vitamins and additional healthy, complex carbohydrates. Granted, the chocolate chips are an indulgence, but the other ingredients more than offset the fat and calories. Besides, when you eat healthy foods most of the time, it's not such a bad thing to have a treat once in a while.

And, if you prepare Daddy's Chocolate Chip and Strawberry Cookie Pancakes just once a month and prepare the recipe using artificial sweetener rather than white sugar, each member of your family will save roughly 150 calories if everyone has two pancakes. That is equal to 1,800 calories a year, or about one entire day's recommended daily allowance (RDA) for calories. In a game of inches, each Daddy's Chocolate Chip and Strawberry Cookie Pancake is like a starting pitcher that goes deep in the game.

Generally, I believe a person should consume a diet that supplies all of the nutrients he or she needs to maintain physical health, which is one of the first steps to creating a healthy lifestyle. For example, by including at least one fruit or vegetable with every meal, a single father goes a long way toward providing the vitamins and fiber in his and his kids' diets that they need to effectively maintain all of the body's functions.

Still, there are instances in which circumstances hinder our ability to get all the vitamins we need. Much of our vitamin D, for example, comes from exposure to sunlight. During the short days of winter, especially in colder climates where people cover their skin with heavy coats, hats, and gloves, there is little opportunity to absorb sunlight and a person can easily become deficient in vitamin D.

# GOLDEN RULE #4:

*Take a fiber supplement along with your vitamins with at least eight ounces of liquid every morning during breakfast.*

Supplements can mitigate deficiencies created by either dietary shortcomings or environmental circumstances. A good quality multivitamin—one that is clinically proven to dissolve prior to leaving the alimentary system—is a very good start. If, at annual checkups, you discover you or your children are lacking in one or more vitamins, specific supplements may be required.

Developing this idea one step further, particularly for the single father, I encourage added fiber in the form of psyllium capsules or fiber mixes, which helps achieve two objectives. First, whether you're having eggs, oatmeal, pancakes, or a bagel for breakfast, fiber taken in the morning with breakfast will help you feel fuller, longer. You'll consume fewer calories in the morning, and you'll be less likely to snack on empty calorie-laden foods before your next meal. The fiber may save you a pancake or half of a bagel, which, over time, will equate to thousands of calories not consumed. Moreover, the extra fiber will help keep your digestive system (note the euphemism) healthy and consistent. It's hard to appreciate the benefit of good digestion if a person hasn't already experienced it, which leads me to The Single Father's Golden Rule #4: *Take a fiber supplement along with your vitamins with at least eight ounces of liquid every morning during breakfast.*

Trust me on this one. You can thank me later.

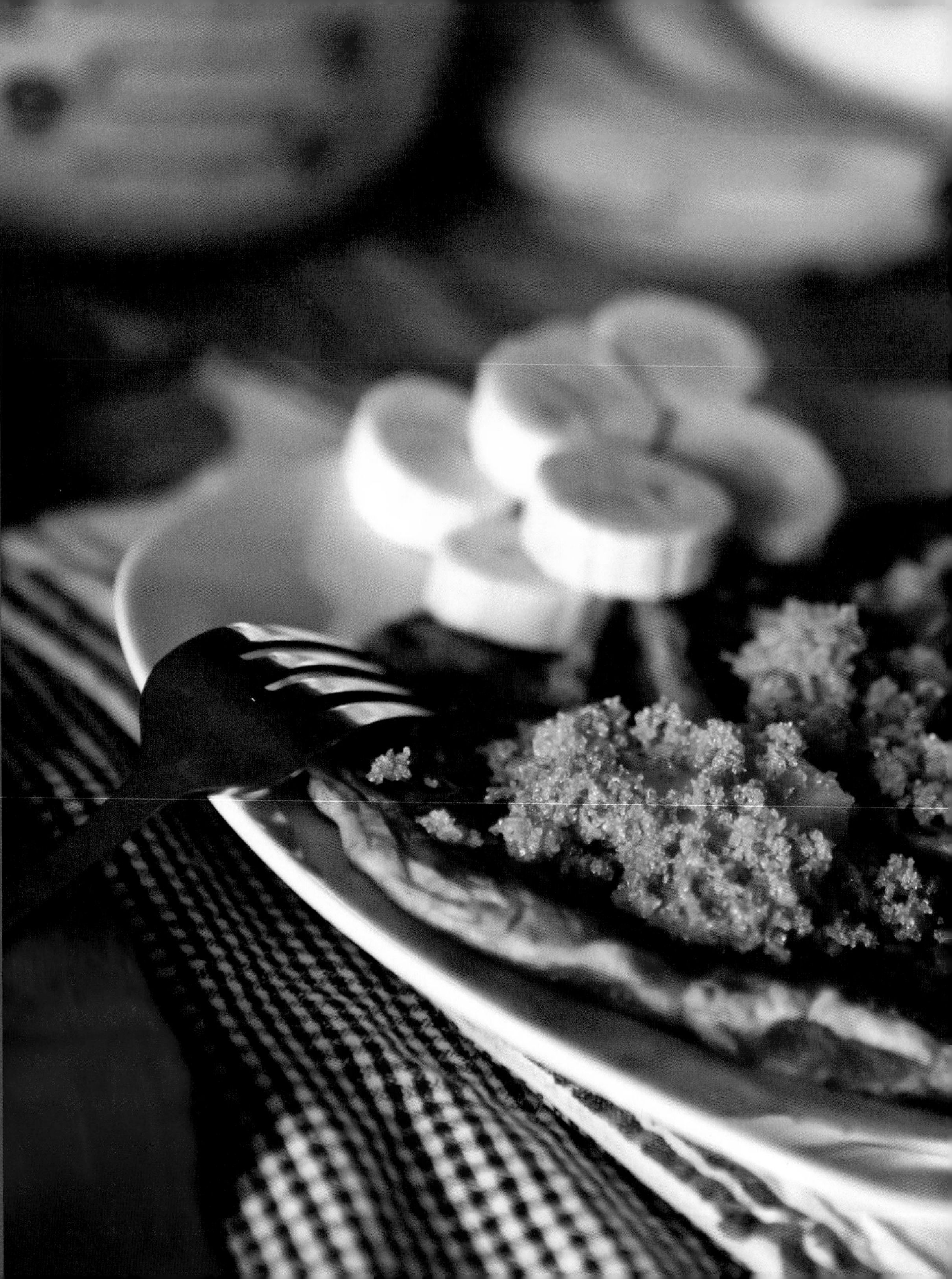

I don't know if it's my training and experience as an efficiency management consultant or just a natural predilection for frugality, but I do my best not to allow much to go to waste. Whether it's oatmeal from yesterday's breakfast, chicken from Sunday night's dinner, or a side of rice that was more than we could eat, I like to reincarnate those ingredients in a new entrée when it's possible.

The ingredient of another of my favorite pancake recipes, one which is a bit easier to make than Dad's Chocolate Chip and Strawberry Cookie Pancakes, makes a tasty use of oatmeal that was left over from the previous morning's breakfast:

## Dad's Favorite Oatmeal Pancakes

| | |
|---|---|
| ⅔ cup whole wheat flour | 2 eggs |
| ⅓ cup soy flour | 2 tablespoons vegetable oil |
| 1 tablespoon baking powder | or melted butter |
| 1 teaspoon salt | 1½ to 2 cups cooked, cooled, |
| 2 cups milk | leftover oatmeal |

Combine the whole wheat flour, soy flour, baking powder, and salt in a bowl, and mix thoroughly. Add the milk, eggs, and 1 tablespoon of vegetable oil, and stir until combined. Then add the oatmeal and stir until any large lumps are removed. Coat a well-heated pan (using medium to medium-high heat depending on the cooktop) with 1 tablespoon of vegetable oil or melted butter. Pour or ladle the batter onto pan. Flip when the pancake is bubbling well. The preparation time is 20 to 25 minutes, and makes about eight large, stick-to-the-ribs pancakes for dad and his three pancake-loving children.

You may have observed that the recipe for Dad's Favorite Oatmeal Pancakes omits any sweetener. In essence, these pancakes are just like oatmeal, but with a crispy, crunchy, tasty flair after being cooked in a pan. For me, just a little bit of butter in the pan is all I need. Because the pancakes are unsweetened, I'm not concerned if the kids "dress them up" a little with brown sugar or honey. Of course, I also like to have raisins, dried blueberries, cherries, cranberries, or even fresh-sliced apples, peaches, or strawberries on the table as a garnish.

As I stressed in the prologue, don't expect exotic, gourmet recipes in *The Single Father's Guide.* Instead, you'll find easy, healthy recipes to help create a healthy, balanced diet for you and your kids. Still, there are a few tricks I've discovered that seem to work better for my recipes, but which may not be quite typical in everyday cooking. As I've already mentioned, I use whole wheat and soy flour in many of my recipes. In addition, because whole wheat and soy flour are denser than white flour, I add a tablespoon of baking powder to the dry ingredients instead of a teaspoon, which is more customary. The additional baking powder, I've found, is necessary to make the pancakes rise the way they're supposed to.

In the cases of both death and divorce, a father has lost something. In the context of a loving relationship with a spouse who has died, the single father not only has to find ways to assist his children with the loss of a mother, but he also must adjust to the emotional and practical loss of his partner and best friend. When a man gets divorced, the conditions for him are similar in some ways. Children still need emotional support to adapt to the change. At the same time, the single father's emotions may range from great relief to great sadness, depending on the circumstances. As Kim Sumner-Mayer puts it:

> Death, while catastrophic, is a clear loss—the spouse is physically and psychologically gone. Whereas divorce is an unclear loss; the spouse is physically still alive, though the relationship and psychological reality is absence or loss. An unclear loss is extremely tormenting to people and often there are no social rituals to ease the transitions brought on by it, so it is extremely stressful.[12]

Both circumstances involve loss, or, if you will, the literal and figurative "death" of a relationship. Regardless of whether the father provided the momentum for the divorce, grief is likely a natural reaction. According to the National Institutes of Health:

> Grief may be triggered by the death of a loved one. People also can experience grief if they have an illness for which there is no cure, or a chronic condition that affects their quality of life. The end of a significant relationship may also cause a grieving process.[13]

There are many constructive ways to process grief. Some of the traditional methods include speaking with a therapist, joining a support group, or meeting with a member of the clergy. Frankly, I don't advocate or oppose any method of grieving. However, there is one central tenet of grieving that I was fortunate enough to learn early enough, which, I believe, helped me more than any mental health professional, group, or clergyperson could have: a friend who's traveled the same road.

I first met Steve White—who went on to write *Family Vacations & Other Hazards of Growing Up*—at the University of Missouri. We were members of the same fraternity, although he was a Kansas City Royals fan while I'd grown up with the St. Louis Cardinals. (The 1985 "I-70" World Series is still a sore subject for me.)

Baseball loyalties run deep, but in spite of our apparent natural incompatibility, Steve and I became friends but drifted apart when my career took me east while Steve returned to Kansas City. When his wife died suddenly, Steve became the only one of my friends or acquaintances among my peers to have lost a spouse. When Lori passed a couple years later, Steve was one of the first of my friends to reach out to provide support.

*I've come to the conclusion that the two most important things in life are good friends and a good bullpen.*
—**Bob Lemon**

A true friend doesn't have to ask permission to offer advice. Frankly, I didn't know what I needed when I became a widower and a single father, but Steve stepped up to the plate. He'd been through it. Steve talked with me about a lot of things, ranging from my own emotional, physical, and spiritual needs, to the expectations of what friends, family, and the community-at-large might have of a widower's behavior, which I was surprised to learn would be one of the issues I'd have to negotiate.

I took away many things from my initial conversation, subsequent exchanges, and correspondence. The most valuable of those things was, undoubtedly, Steve's mantra, *There is no wrong way to grieve as long as you don't hurt anyone in the process,* which I've adopted as The Single Father's Golden Rule #5. There is precious little I've learned, before or after, that has been more valuable to me.

When Steve said, "There is no wrong way to grieve as long as you don't hurt anyone in the process," he may as well have been speaking a dead

## GOLDEN RULE #5:

*There is no wrong way to grieve as long as you don't hurt anyone in the process.*

language. I had no idea what he meant. When I asked him to give me an example, he shed light on a great number of things with which I'd have to contend outside of the strict realm of parenthood and homemaking.

Whether a man is divorced or widowed, people—specifically, your family, your ex-wife's or late wife's family, your religious community, and your neighbors, to name a few—have expectations of your behavior. Those expectations may come from a sincere concern for your welfare, or from moral judgments people impose on you. Regardless of the reasons, grief is a very personal emotion and others will have their own conceptions of how a man in your position should behave. Many of those people, however, will not have experienced the things that you have, and none of those people, clearly, are you. What works for someone else, may not—almost certainly will not—work for you.

When Steve offered me his guidance, he didn't say, "Do this." He did say, "Do what you need to do to make yourself whole again and able to take care of yourself and the people who depend on you." In other words, if you believe it would help you to participate in a support group, then, by all means, do so. If you don't think a support group will help, then don't go. And no one else can tell you when it will be right time to start dating and whether or not you should get remarried. Those decisions are personal, in spite of people sharing their own opinions.

The qualification, ". . . as long as you don't hurt anyone in the process," is of particular importance. When others depend on you, especially children, there really is no place for destructive behavior. Turning to alcohol, using unprescribed or illegal drugs, taking unreasonable risks, and indulging in other self-destructive behaviors will have negative, and perhaps tragic, results.

## Oven-Baked Bacon, Scrambled Eggs, and Warm Cinnamon Apples

1 pound thick-sliced bacon

6 eggs

2 to 3 sliced apples, with the skin
   left on -

2 tablespoons sugar or sugar
   substitute

1 pinch dill

1 tablespoon vegetable oil

½ teaspoon salt

½ teaspoon cinnamon

¼ teaspoon pepper

⅛ cup water

Preheat the oven to 250°. On a large baking pan, lay the bacon strips side to side. Place the pan in the oven and cook for 50 minutes. In a small saucepan, mix the sliced apples, 2 tablespoons of sugar or sugar substitute, ¼ teaspoon of salt, ½ teaspoon of cinnamon, and ⅛ cup of water. Bring the mixture to a boil, then cover and reduce the heat to low; simmer for about 15 minutes or until mixture thickens. In a bowl, combine the eggs with ½ tablespoon of the vegetable oil, a pinch of dill, ¼ teaspoon of salt, and ¼ teaspoon of pepper, and beat until mixed. Coat a frying pan with ½ tablespoon of vegetable oil and heat using medium or medium-high heat. Pour eggs into the frying pan; stir gently with a spatula until cooked. Total preparation time is about 75 minutes, but the crispy bacon is worth the wait. A great start for a relaxed dad and his three kids.

The sauced apple wedges in the Oven-Baked Bacon, Scrambled Eggs, and Warm Cinnamon Apples recipe very nicely complement the thick-cut, oven-baked bacon, especially if you can find apple-smoked bacon. That's not the only benefit to this recipe, though. The fact that the bacon needs to cook at the low temperature for an hour provides you, Dad, time for a brisk two- or three-mile walk to clear your head and get some exercise at the same time. Although I don't necessarily advocate leaving the house while something is cooking, leaving the bacon in the oven is akin to leaving a chicken in a crock pot to slow cook all day. Besides, if one of your children is a little older and knows his or her way around the kitchen, you'll have someone to keep an eye on the bacon's progress while you're walking.

With some regularity, you'll need time to clear your head, catch your breath, or just get away for a few minutes. You may be frustrated with something at work, and you'll unconsciously bring that frustration home. At every age, your children will challenge you in ways you may not have imagined, from the good-natured, trouble-making toddler to the brooding teenager who is testing his or her limits. Take a step back. Take a little time. The brisk walk, especially if you make it part of your routine, will be a natural way to clear your mind, reassess your situation, get some exercise, and relieve stress.

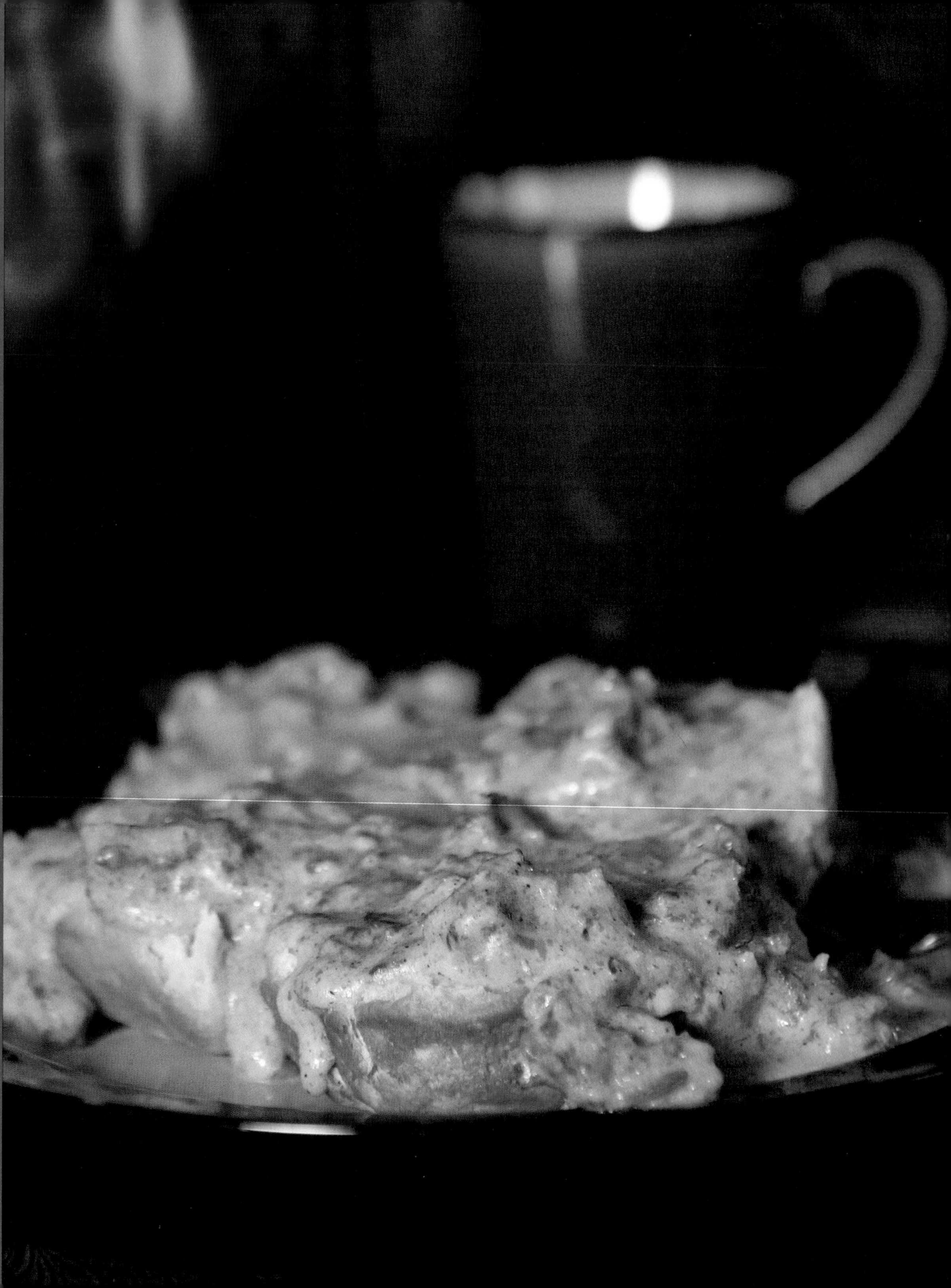

# Missouri-Style Gravy 'n' Biscuits

1 pound ground breakfast sausage

1 sweet onion, diced

1 garlic clove, crushed, or ¼ teaspoon garlic powder

6 cups milk

2 heaping tablespoons whole wheat flour

½ teaspoon pepper

1 pinch salt (optional)

8 biscuits (either packaged or from a can) or 8 pieces of toast

In a large, high-sided frying pan, add diced sweet onion, garlic, and ground breakfast sausage. Cook on medium heat until the sausage is thoroughly browned. Remove the sausage from pan and drain the grease. To the pan, add the milk and ½ teaspoon pepper. Warm on medium heat, and sift 2 tablespoons of whole wheat flour into the milk while stirring gently. Continue to stir for 3 to 5 minutes until thickened. Stir in browned sausage and onion. If you're using brown-and-serve biscuits, follow the baking directions on the can, or toast 8 pieces of bread. (You can substitute chicken or turkey sausage for pork sausage; soy, almond, or rice milk for cow's milk; and wheat toast for white toast). Feeds the trail boss and his three little cowboys and cowgirls.

No doubt, you'll have your hands full on many mornings, Dad. Even if you share custody of your children, some of the time you'll be the project manager to get the kids out of bed, dressed, fed, lunches made, and on the bus. Of course, older children provide their own unique challenges and opportunities: small children, small problems; big children, big problems.

Regardless, there will just be some days that you don't even have the two minutes to prepare and eat a healthy smoothie. Don't fret, but be prepared.

Every couple of weeks, grab a dozen bagels. Rather than buying plain bagels, though, choose bagels that have a little substance. Blueberry, cheese, cinnamon-raisin, pumpernickel, and whole wheat, among others, often contain fewer calories, offer a variety of tastes, and provide nutritional benefits not found in the plain kind. Then, take five minutes to slice the bagels in half, place four to six of the sliced bagels in a large zipper-lock freezer bag, and they're ready to toast on the morning after the power surge that reset your alarm clock or when you find indisputable evidence that your golden retriever wasn't able to digest the chocolate bar your three-year-old son fed her the previous evening. Serve toasted bagels with almond butter, butter, cream cheese, hazelnut spread, or peanut butter, and garnish with two or three apple slices, banana slices, grapefruit chunks, grapes, orange wedges, or strawberries.

If you don't even have time for that quick breakfast solution, there's nothing wrong with sending your kids out the door with a granola bar and a piece of fruit in hand. Even when the pressure is on, you can feel good about the fact that you were able to begin your day—and theirs—with a healthy, filling breakfast.

Nice start, Dad.

# THE LONG RELIEVER
## LUNCH

If a single dad works in an office, he may have his lunch with his coworkers or with clients. If he's self-employed and works at home, he may just grab something quick. How and what you eat during the middle of the day isn't just important to maintaining a healthy lifestyle for you and you kids—it's critical.

Think of lunch as the long reliever in your bullpen. Any baseball manager can tell you that in a close game the quality of the long and middle relief is the difference between winning and losing both the game and the season. You don't need me to tell you that every day in the life of a single father is a "close game." If the guy with the ball regularly blows the lead or fails to keep the game close in the middle innings, then the losses really start to pile up.

> *No matter how good you are, you're going to lose one-third of your games. No matter how bad you are you're going to win one-third of your games. It's the other third that makes the difference.*
> —**Tommy Lasorda**

Tommy Lasorda's quote rings true for the single father and for the "players" on his "team." Eating poorly at lunch, whether at home or on the road, can undo much of the other terrific things you do nutritionally and physically. According to a recent study, "Right now, 32 percent of men and 34 percent of women are obese.

Those numbers are projected to rise to 43 and 42 percent in 2020, nudging up toward half of all people,"[14] and that really drives home the point about the importance of a good lunch.

The time-honored "drive-thru" lunch at McDonalds, consisting of a Big Mac, a medium order of fries, and a medium soft drink, adds up to 1,130 calories and 48 grams of fat (74 percent of the RDA), and 151 grams of carbohydrates—or 50 percent of the RDA![15] In terms of a 2,000- or 2,500-calorie diet, your drive-thru lunch is either almost half or more than half of your caloric intake (along with all the fat and carbs), and you haven't even taken into account breakfast, dinner, or snack!

Let me be clear. I enjoy fast-food restaurants like McDonalds and Burger King, and I think they're great for their convenience and for some of their lower-calorie, healthy items. I also think it's not such a bad thing to enjoy some of the indulgence items, like a Big Mac or a Whopper, once in a while. But a regular disregard for the high amounts of calories, fat, and carbohydrates in many fast-food items is at best unwise, and at worst dangerously unhealthy.

For your school-age children who have the opportunity to buy lunch at school, the situation is a little different. According to one study, "[National School Lunch Program] participants are more likely than non-participants to consume vegetables, milk and milk products, and meat and other protein-rich foods, both at lunch and over 24 hours; they also consume less soda and/or fruit drinks."[16] However—and this is a "C'mon Man!" question—have you actually seen the way school lunches *look* these days?

I'll note here that there is a movement these days to make school lunch offerings healthier and more appetizing, with fresh ingredients coming from local producers. We all look forward to the day when these lunches become the norm.

Meanwhile, if buying school lunches is a necessity for your kids—maybe even a godsend—the trick is to try to teach your offspring, early and often, how to make healthy choices.

Those caveats aside, while it may be true that kids who eat school lunches do, in fact, eat more vegetables, dairy, and meat and drink healthier beverages, most of the time you can still do better! First, "more likely" could just mean *a little* more likely. Second, and with all due respect to all the hard-working cafeteria ladies out there, the lunches served in our schools can be extremely unappetizing. In my experience, white bread, pasty spaghetti, overcooked vegetables, and smallish, not-so-fresh fruits are the standard. Even the cafeteria pizza served on "Pizza Friday," which I fondly recall from my own formative years, features disappointingly little cheese and is often burnt and cold.

My solution for the single father and his clan of little learners is . . . the figurative brown bag. Pack lunches! When you and your kids bring the lunch that you've made, you positively influence the eating habits you as a family develop when you are away from home, you provide a balanced meal consistent with an overall nutritional diet, and you make the lunch more appetizing, at least compared to the school cafeteria's offerings. Here's a template for a standard "brown bag" lunch:

- **Sandwich:** Use whole wheat or whole grain bread, which provides a lower-calorie, more filling, and digestively beneficial alternative to white bread. It's not such a big deal if you make peanut butter and jelly (or an alternative like hazelnut spread and jam) occasionally as long as you also regularly make sandwiches with lean cold cuts and cheese, too. For flavor, obviously, add condiments, like mustard, catsup, or mayonnaise, in moderation, and garnishes, like lettuce, tomato, or onion, in surplus.

**Fruit/Vegetable:** An apple, an orange, or a banana is always a great, practical supplement to a lunch. In season, fruits like cherries, grapes, nectarines, peaches, and plums are equally good and provide variety. A container filled with baby carrots, sliced celery, cauliflower, or even baby pickles served with or without a little dressing for dipping also fits the bill. Even a fruit cup, which may not be quite as advantageous as fresh fruit or vegetables, is better than no fruit or vegetable at all!

**Crunchy:** Not including a "crunchy" item is really all right. You and your kids don't need them. If you prefer something crunchy and salty in your lunch, though, consider a buying larger bags of flavored mini rice cakes, healthy crackers, nuts, or even a few pretzels, and packing them into smaller snack bags. If you insist on the snack bags of things like potato chips or corn chips, look for the baked varieties rather than the fried to save a few grams of fat and calories. You could certainly do worse!

**Dessert:** A couple of cookies or a snack cake is not so bad once in a while. Even in terms of cookies, some are better than others. Fig or fruit-filled cookies are probably better than chocolate chip cookies that are chock full of butter or shortening, sugar, and other empty calories. In general, however, a granola bar is often sweet enough to punctuate the meal, and, again, will stick with you longer than a Twinkie!

Of course, variety is the spice of life, and, conveniently, many school cafeterias and office lunch rooms provide access to a microwave oven to heat

brown-bagged entrees. Every now and then, replace the sandwich with a piece of chicken left over from the previous night's dinner or with soup packed in a microwave-safe container. You might even put a couple of pieces of Thursday night's pizza in Friday's lunch!

## Father's Recipe Chicken Rice Soup

1 "what's left of last night's chicken"

8 cups water

2 cups cooked rice

4 whole carrots, sliced

2 stalks celery, diced

2 cloves garlic, crushed

1 tablespoon salt

1 teaspoon pepper

Add 8 cups of water and leftover chicken in a pot. Simmer on low or low-medium setting for an hour. Let it cool. (To get 2 cups of cooked rice, add 1 cup of rice to 2 cups of boiling water, along with 1 tablespoon of butter, and a pinch of salt in a saucepan. Reduce heat to low and simmer covered for 20 minutes.) Remove the meat from the chicken bones. Keep the meat, discard the bones. Add cooked rice, sliced carrots, diced celery, crushed garlic, salt, and pepper. Bring the mixture to a boil, and cook on low heat for 15 minutes. Serve hot and season to taste. The total preparation time is 75 minutes, and makes a great lunch for the bodies and minds of one single father and his three kids.

It's not just single fathers who have to deal with children who are picky when it comes to food. Except for the lucky few whose child will eat anything his or her parent puts on the table, fathers everywhere fight the Battle of Brussels Sprouts or the Assault on Asparagus almost every day.

In the traditional two-parent family, a division of labor between a husband and a wife clearly creates efficiencies in the home. The dividend of those efficiencies is the most valuable of assets: time. So, the finicky little eater may find the parent who prepares the meals in an "intact" family more likely to concede certain menu items for the sake of family harmony. For the single father, frankly, time is not an abundant resource.

Think about your day. You might have to make breakfast in between your shower and getting the kids up and dressed, then find time to make a quick, filling, and healthy lunch to take to school, and later have to coordinate dinner with homework, track practice, and a parent-teacher conference. You don't have the luxury to cook-to-order. In most cases, you cannot afford the time to make a tofu burger for one child and chicken for another—even on a weekend—which is why some of the recipes below are perfect for making (and eating) when you're all together. You're in charge of the team so you get to make the call, which is the cornerstone for The Single Father's Golden Rule #6: *Dad is NOT a short-order cook!*

## GOLDEN RULE #6:

### *Dad is NOT a short-order cook!*

# Dad's Microwave Stuffed Spuds

4 to 5 raw potatoes

3 cups broccoli

3 cups shredded cheddar cheese

4 tablespoons butter

1 teaspoon salt

½ teaspoon pepper

4 slices cooked bacon (optional)

Wash the potatoes and prick each one thoroughly with a fork to allow expansion of moisture without having the potato explode. (I learned about that the hard way.) Place the potatoes in a microwave oven at a high setting, and cook for approximately 7 minutes, then turn them over and cook for 7 more minutes. Remove the potatoes. Place the broccoli in microwave oven, program to high setting, and cook for approximately 5 minutes. While the broccoli is cooking, open up the potatoes just enough to stuff them and put one on each plate. On each potato, add a tablespoon of butter and a pinch each of salt and pepper. If you have bacon, perhaps left over from the morning's breakfast, crush it into small pieces and add to each potato. Once the broccoli is cooked, spread ¾ cup on each potato and add another pinch of salt to each. Finally, drizzle ¾ cup of shredded cheddar onto each potato, and then microwave each potato again for approximately 90 seconds or until the cheese is melted. The total preparation time is about 20 minutes, and each stuffed spud will give a single father and his three children the energy to run the bases for the rest of the afternoon.

Just because you don't have the time to prepare à la carte meals doesn't mean one or more of your children will stop being particular about their meals.

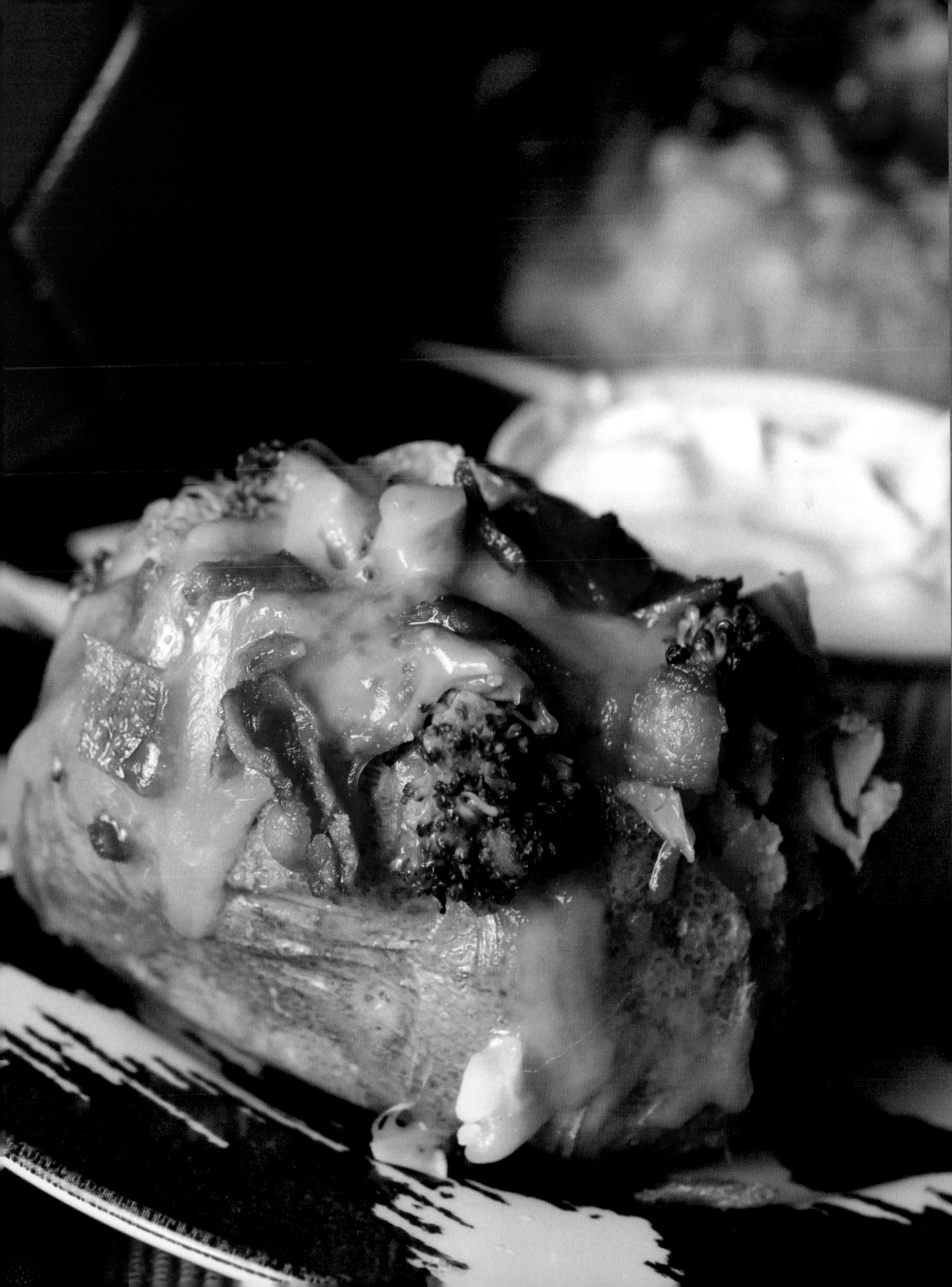

At the same time, a child who doesn't like green vegetables or red meat or dairy will not get the nutrients his or her body needs if an important component of a balanced diet is omitted. Moreover, the picky child who regularly fails to eat one or more vegetables at meal times risks developing poor eating habits as an adult. These issues present a real dilemma for the single father.

*It's a round ball and a round bat, and you got to hit it square.*
—Pete Rose

To remedy this situation in my family, I've instituted the "eat the food I make" clause, but I've included a great deal of variety in our diets to preclude the child who doesn't like green vegetables, for example, from having to eat them every day. In addition, I've used a "pull, not push" technique to consistently apply the "eat the food I make" clause. In short, "pull, not push" means I don't force my children to eat the food I've made. Rather, when one of my children asserts his or her independence and boldly states, "I don't like this! I'm not

eating it," I don't make a challenge. I don't say, "Eat the food I made!" That would be the equivalent of trying to push a boulder up a perpetually rising incline. You might make a little occasional progress, but, in the long run, you'll get tired of pushing and the boulder will roll back over you! Instead, I respond, "That's fine. You don't have to eat. But before you can have a snack or dessert—assuming a healthy dessert is on the menu—you have to eat your dinner." Then, without argument or debate, lead by example and simply continue eating.

# Apple Cinnamon Pie

5 medium to large apples
2 ready-made, packaged pie shells
1 cup brown sugar and artificial sweetener (50-50 mixture)
2 tablespoons lemon juice

1 heaping tablespoon whole wheat flour
1 tablespoon cinnamon
1 teaspoon salt
½ teaspoon vanilla extract
1 pinch allspice

Preheat the oven to 350°. Core five apples and dice into large pieces with the skin on. In a large mixing bowl, add diced apples, the brown sugar/artificial sweetener mixture, 2 tablespoons of lemon juice, 1 tablespoon of whole wheat flour, 1 tablespoon of cinnamon, 1 teaspoon of salt, ½ teaspoon of vanilla extract, and 1 pinch of allspice. Mix thoroughly. In a pie pan, place 1 pie shell on the bottom of the pan and mold to the pan. Add the apple mixture. Put 1 pie shell atop the apple mixture, and crimp at the edge with the bottom pie shell. Use a knife to make slits on top to vent. Bake for 45 minutes or until the pie shell crust is golden brown. Makes a great dessert for three great kids and their dad, if he has eaten his dinner.

If you have only one child on the team, you can play the man-to-man defense. With more than one, though, you've got to play zone. Among my three kids, there is always at least one who likes everything on the plate. Usually, the second will go along with the majority whether he or she likes everything or not. In almost every case, the third who made the challenge and wasn't rewarded with the desired reaction will simply give in to the majority to be included with the rest of the family.

For the single father of one child, the process will most likely be even easier. In many ways, perhaps even all ways, you are the entire world to your child at that moment. Your little lady or gentleman both loves and depends on you. If you are consistent and confident while remaining affectionate and assuring, your child will want to emulate your behavior. In those cases when the child becomes fussy with food, remain patient and firm. Remember, it is important for both you and your child to eat a balanced diet, and you're the parent!

## St. Louis-Style Thin-Crust Sausage and Onion Pizza

2 cups whole wheat flour

⅛ cup sugar substitute

1 tablespoon dried basil

1 teaspoon garlic powder

1 teaspoon salt

1 heaping tablespoon dry active
   yeast

¾ cup water

2 tablespoons extra virgin olive oil

2 tomatoes

3 tablespoons grated parmesan
   cheese

¾ pound sliced provolone cheese

1 pound ground sausage

1 onion, diced

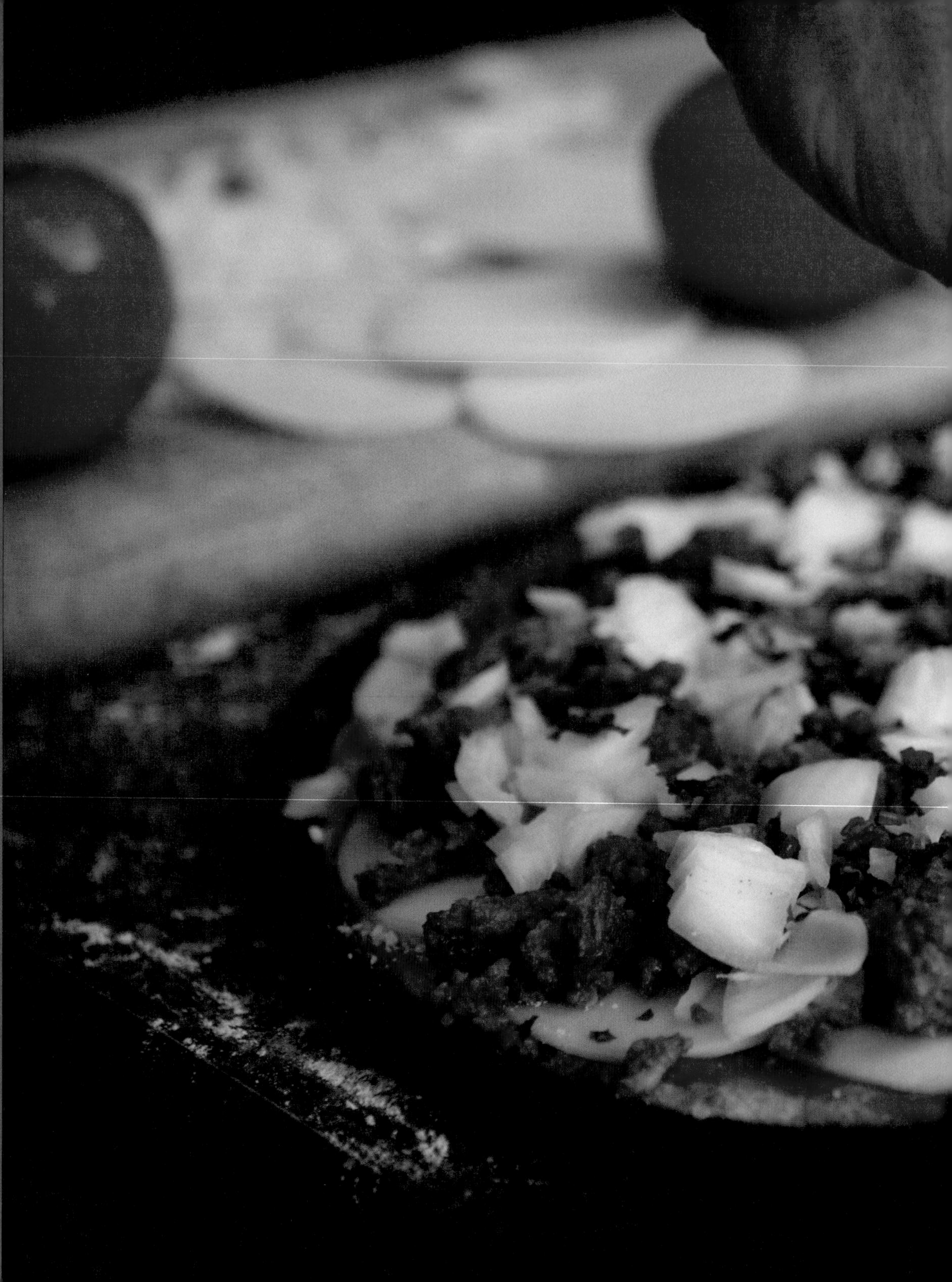

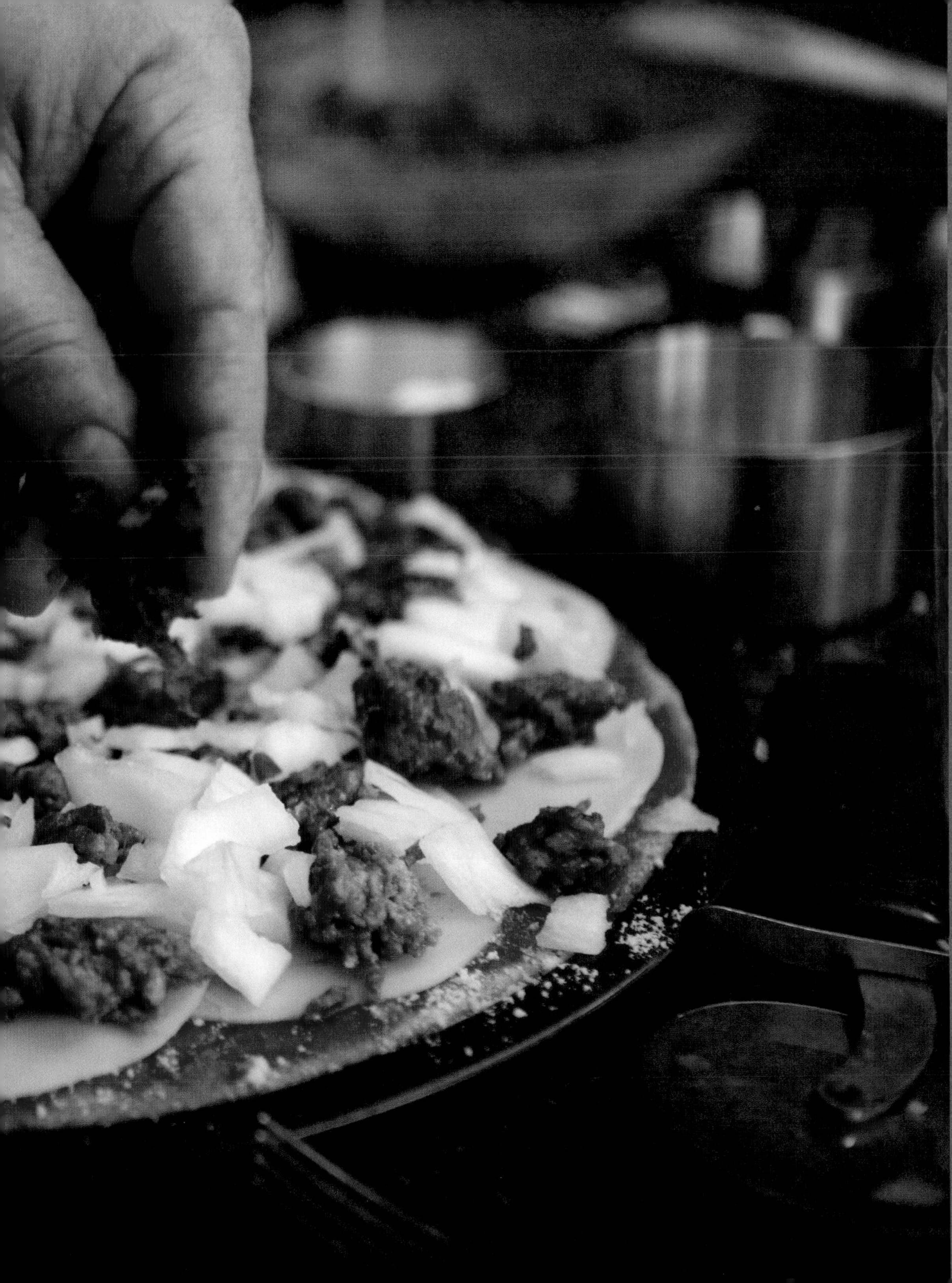

In a bowl, combine the flour, sugar substitute, basil, garlic, salt, and yeast. Mix thoroughly. Heat ¾ cup of water in microwave until the temperature is approximately 130°. (Use a food thermometer to estimate water temperature.) Pour the heated water and two tablespoons of olive oil into the dry mixture, and combine and knead thoroughly. Cover and put in a warm place and let the dough rise for about one hour. Preheat the oven to 400°.

In a frying pan, brown the sausage over medium heat, and drain the grease. Using a knife or food processor, chop the onion coarsely. After the dough has risen, push it down with your fingers. Dust a large cookie sheet with flour and roll the dough onto the cookie sheet until the thickness is approximately ¼" to ⅜". Prick the rolled dough thoroughly with a fork to prevent bubbling while cooking.

Cut out the stems from the tomatoes and squeeze out the seeds and moisture. With a knife or a food processor, chop the tomatoes coarsely, and spread evenly over the dough. Dust with grated parmesan cheese. Lay slices of provolone cheese evenly over the tomatoes and parmesan. Finally, spread browned sausage and chopped onion over the top of the cheese. Place in a preheated oven and cook for 12 to 16 minutes until the cheese is golden brown. Slice into squares, St. Louis-style, and enjoy. Total preparation time is 75 to 90 minutes, and is the perfect weekend afternoon cooking project for a single dad and kids.

In the early eras of human development, it's likely that primitive males who got back to the camp quickest after a hunt would have first access to females and thus a better chance of propagating their genes.[17] Perhaps a man's reluctance to ask for driving directions is connected to this evolutionarily selected trait; admitting he is lost is like conceding his manhood. Of course, personal global positioning systems will probably make that time-honored male attribute obsolete, so the jokes about how men would rather be lost and late than ask for directions will be completely missed by future generations.

There may not be a connection between a man's disinclination to ask for driving directions and his unwillingness to ask for help when he needs it, but failing to do the latter may have damaging results for the single father and his family.

Most conversations—in their subject matter, tone, and purpose—tend to be different among men and women. Male bonding is different from female bonding. It just is. While men discuss sports, politics, and power equipment to demonstrate knowledge, wit, or dominance, in my experience, women focus on topics and strategies that develop cooperation, community, and support. Moms share parenting ideas with one another and use these conversations to resolve questions and quandaries about parenthood. It is during these mysterious conversation klatches—which form spontaneously at playgroups, after PTA meetings, or at the local playground—that many of the secrets of raising children are addressed.

*Every day is a new opportunity. You can build on yesterday's success or put its failures behind and start over again. That is the way life is, with a new game every day, and that's the way baseball is.*
—**Bob Feller**

If there is any doubt that women and men interact and bond differently, just answer the question, Dad, when was the last time you asked one of your buddies, "What's the best way to get rid of diaper rash?"

Don't fret. Well, maybe you can fret a little, because the solution to your parenting knowledge deficiency involves actual cooperative conversation and can be summarized in The Single Father's Golden Rule #7: *Make friends with mothers of your children's friends, and then be a friend . . . a platonic friend.*

## GOLDEN RULE #7:

*Make friends with mothers of your children's friends, and then be a friend . . . a platonic friend.*

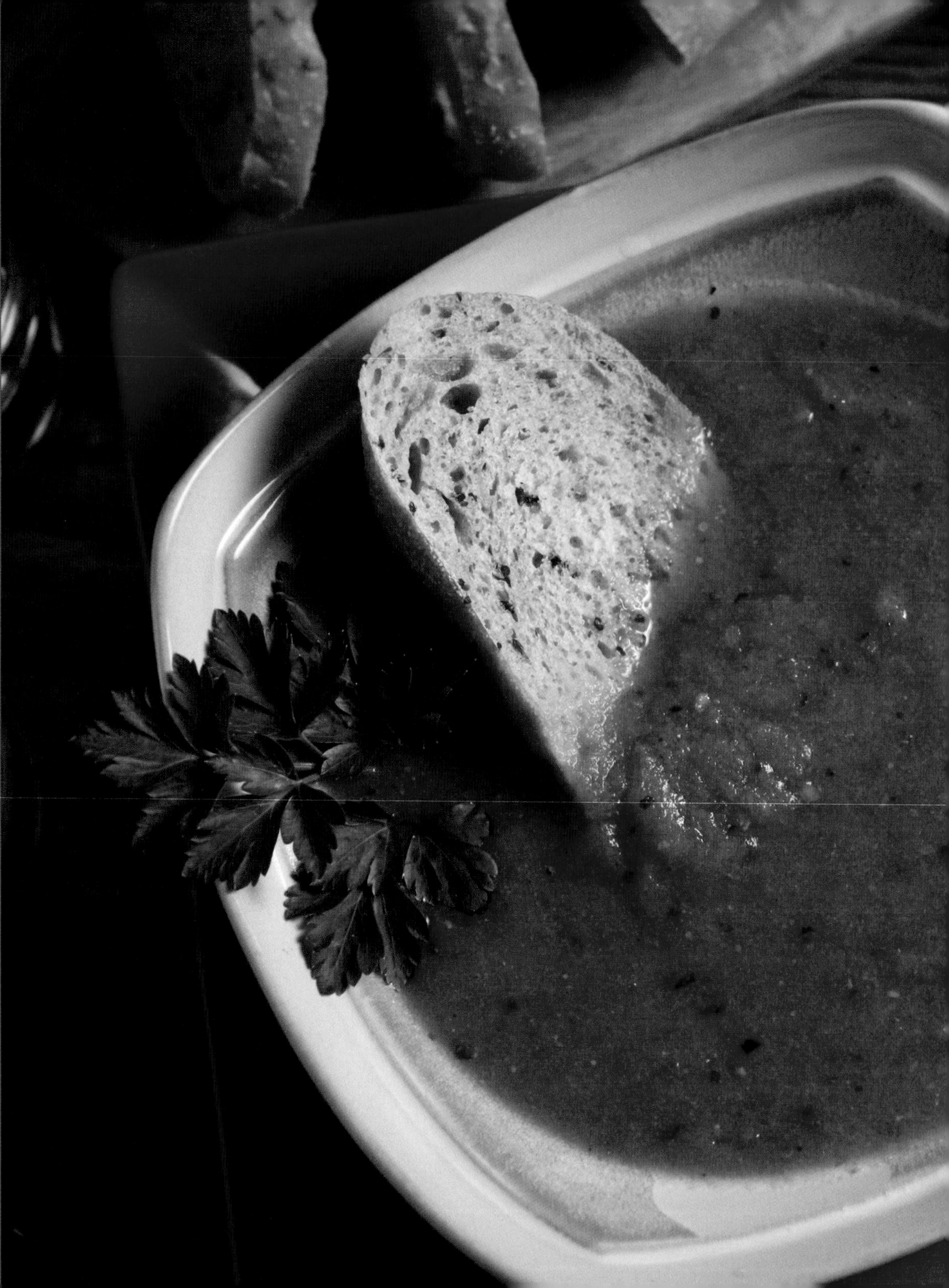

# Dad's Garden Harvest Tomato Soup

| | |
|---|---|
| 8 to 10 medium-sized tomatoes | 1 cup water |
| 2 packets of onion soup mix or ½ diced onion with 1 large (or 4 small) beef bouillon cube(s) | 1 cup milk |
| | ¼ teaspoon pepper |
| | 2 tablespoons chopped basil |

In a large saucepan or a small soup pot, add 1 cup of water, chopped basil, and either 2 packets of dried onion soup mix or half a diced onion and 1 large (or 4 small) beef bouillon cube(s), and bring to a boil. Cone-cut the stems from the tomatoes, then squeeze each tomato gently to expel the seeds. Place the stemmed and seeded tomatoes and 1 cup of milk into a blender and mix at a low speed until pureed. Add tomato puree and ¼ teaspoon of pepper to the soup pot, and stir. Turn the burner to medium-low and simmer until onions are tender. Serve with crackers or whole wheat rolls to three hungry children and a single dad on a brisk, autumn football Saturday or Sunday.

It really is a new ball game, and no other person knows the rules of that new ball game better than the people who've already been playing it for a while. For the single father who sincerely makes an effort to do the best for his children, he will often find others—especially the sympathetic mothers of his children's friends—more than willing to help.

Within a few months after I became a single father, I began to worry a little about my son socializing with other children. Considering he was only about a year old, my concern didn't reach the level of urgency, but I had seen my wife involve each of our older daughters in playgroups with other moms and their children. We'd even enrolled both of my girls in programs like Gymboree and Kindermusik, in which I'd also been fortunate enough to participate. It bothered me to think that my son wouldn't have those same opportunities.

During the nearly two years we lived in our little rural New York village, I'd met some of the friends my wife had made and became friends with others in the community who'd been supportive during her illness. Considering that many of those people had much in common with us, at least in terms of age and outlook, it wasn't terribly surprising to discover that many also had infants about the same age as my son. I reached out to nearly a dozen mothers of those children and suggested that we start a playgroup. About half responded and contacted a couple of their own friends. For almost four years, until our kids started kindergarten, I met this group of mothers and their children at one of our homes every week during the school year. My son met other children with whom he learned to play, share, and resolve minor conflicts. Those children continue to be among his friends today. Equally as important, I listened, asked questions, and learned ways to handle some of the common and uncommon challenges of parenthood.

Some of the "playgroup mothers" have become family friends, and I continue to see the moms from the playgroup at school functions, little league games, or birthday parties. When we run into each other, I still look to them for advice about the challenges I face as a parent of both adolescent girls and a growing boy. I'm sure I'll continue to seek their counsel as my older children grow toward young womanhood and my son deals with the challenges of social interactions, academics, and health in the shadow of a single-father environment.

The platonic female friends (PFFs) I've made during my single-father journey have not been limited to just the playgroup mothers. I've become friends with neighbors, parents of the children in my kids' classes, and people with whom I've had common interests. As it would be with any of my male friends, the level of familiarity I have with my PFFs ranges from just being sociable to sharing more openly about my life. As far as I know, my relationships with my PFFs have never been a source of apprehension on the part of their husbands. Frankly, I've never given any reason for them to be. Some of my romantic interests, however, have felt differently.

In general, there is nothing wrong with maintaining an informal friendship with a PFF. In fact, fostering such connections can benefit both parties, especially the single father who can ask questions and receive straight answers about some of the more sensitive matters a parent faces, such as dealing with adolescent daughters or handling behavioral problems.

*Romance is a lot like baseball.*
*It's not whether you win or lose.*
*It's how you play the game.*
—**Tagline for the film** *Bull Durham*

Of course, there is a difference between being informal and emotionally intimate, though. Informality suggests the avoidance of pretenses, which is valuable in any relationship. On the other hand, emotional intimacy includes the essence of a person's being that isn't shared with just anyone. As long as a guy saves the intimate conversations for his romantic partner, then he'll stay well within the foul pole. If he does, but his romantic interest continues to feel resentful, then it may be appropriate to take an objective look at the viability of the romantic connection.

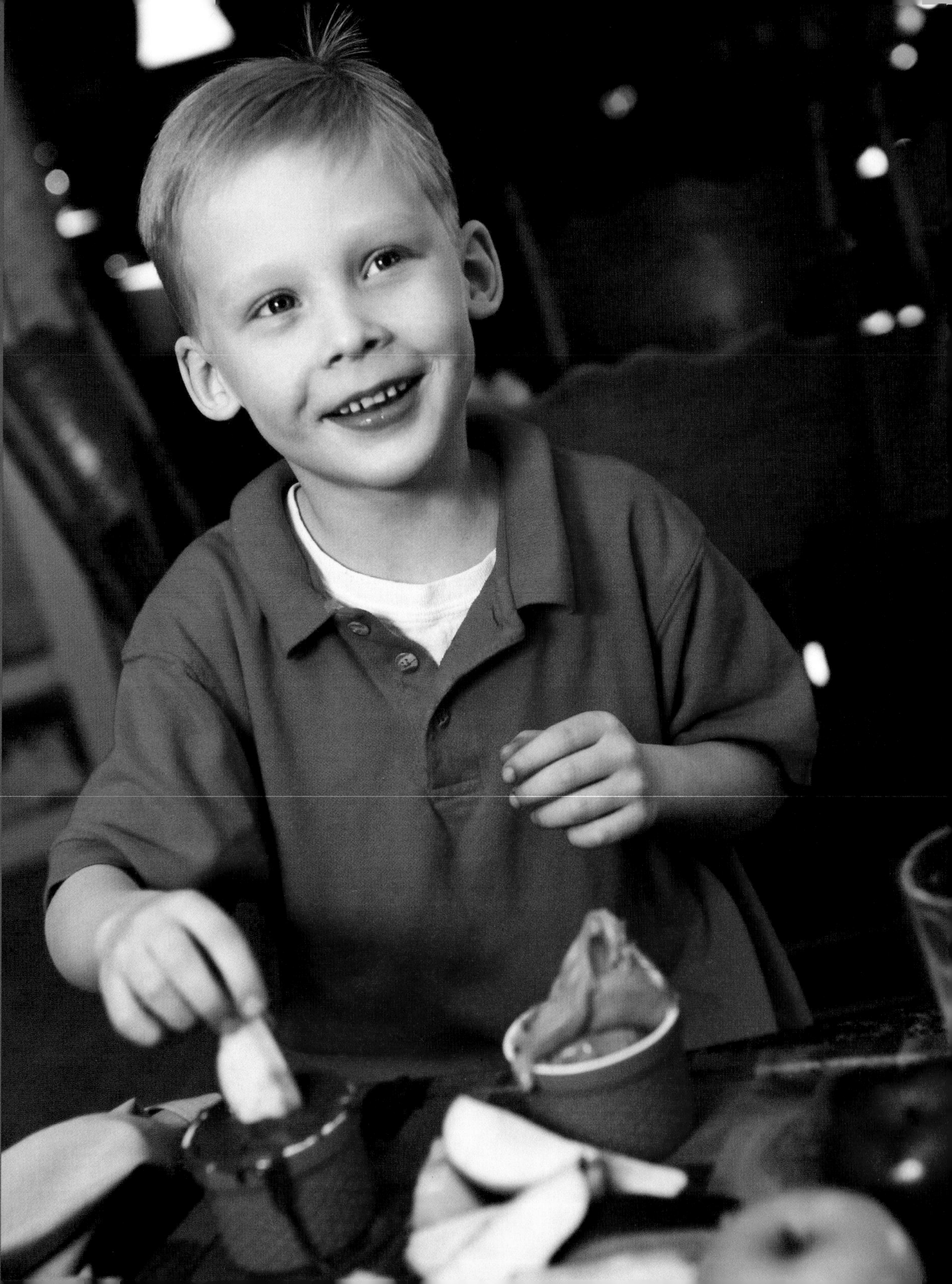

# YOUR UTILITY PLAYER
## SNACKS

## Daddy's Dippin' Apples

2 apples, sliced
1 heaping tablespoon of creamy
    peanut or almond butter

1 heaping tablespoon of
    hazelnut spread

With a knife or an apple corer, cut apples into 12 to 16 wedges. Plop heaping tablespoons of both creamy peanut butter and hazelnut spread on a plate with the sliced apples. Dip apples and devour. Preparation time is about 90 seconds, including opening jars and getting a plate out of the cupboard. Makes a fast and healthy after-school snack for three young scholars and their proud papa.

Switching from chips to apples as a snack is like a clean-up hitter turning on a hanging curve ball. It's a home run every time. To make a positive impact on everyone's health, you have to make the switch consistently. To be consistent, you'll need to start with your trip to the grocery store.

*In baseball,*
*you don't know nothing.*
—Yogi Berra

Each of us has begun our role as the single father carrying different experiences, various skills, and diverse knowledge. In other words, I know some single fathers haven't spent much time in a grocery store other than, perhaps, to visit the snack, soft drink, or beer aisles.

No problem—except that it's generally a good idea to avoid all three of these aisles. With few exceptions, the products you'll find there will be nutritionally suspect: some combination of high calorie, high fat, and/or high carbohydrate. As Dr. Arthur Agatston, a preventive cardiologist writes, "The reality is, when you stop buying junk and purchase only nutrient-rich, high-quality food, you'll be surprised by how far you can stretch your grocery dollars.[18]" As such, The Single Father's Golden Rule #8 is: *If you don't bring junk food home in your grocery bags, you and your children won't eat it!*

Now that we've got that out of the way, let's move on to the actual process of buying groceries that will help to sustain a healthy lifestyle and happy children without busting your budget!

In just about any part of the country, single fathers will have access to more than one option for groceries. For the sake of simplicity, I'll classify grocery stores into two categories. Category #1 is your standard supermarket chain, like Dierbergs, HEB, IGA, Kroger, Shop 'n Save, ShopRite, Stop & Shop, and Wegmans, or your local, independently owned grocery store. Category #2 includes no-frills discount grocery stores, like Aldi, BJ's, Costco, Sam's Club, and perhaps even Walmart Supercenters, where items can be bought in bulk, at significant discounts, or both. Category #1 stores generally stock national brands that you may prefer or have items that you cannot find at the discount stores. Category #2 stores often feature closeouts or overstocked items from suppliers and distributors, as well as good prices on commodity staples like fruits, grains, and vegetables. In my experience, there is a value in choosing one store from each category to fill your family's monthly grocery basket.

# GOLDEN RULE #8:

*If you don't bring junk food home in your grocery bags, you and your children won't eat it!*

First, choose a Category #1 store where you can conveniently shop when you are going to or coming from your regular destinations. If your grocery store is on the way to your workplace, your gym, or your kids' school, then you won't have to make a special trip; that's a time saver, and time really is money! Essentially every Category #1 has a rewards program. Sign up! Not only will you have access to special discounts that the grocery store reserves exclusively for shoppers who use the store's rewards card, but you're also likely to receive special discount offers in the mail when the store needs to boost sales for the ending of a fiscal period or when the store's buyers make a big purchase. In short, the Category #1 grocery store will reward loyalty if you are a regular shopper.

Category #1 grocery stores also invest a great deal of money in advertising. To make sure their advertising dollars are providing enough of a benefit compared to the cost, the Category #1 store will frequently include "loss-leader" coupons in weekly circulars or the local newspaper. A loss-leader coupon is an offer for a certain item in which there is little, if any, profit, just to get a shopper into the store. For their customers' convenience, Category #1 stores will usually advertise in the same papers on the same days each week. Loss leaders I've seen include bargains like a 5-pound bag of white

potatoes for 99¢, a 1-pound bag of store brand baby carrots for 28¢, or a 5-ounce can of white tuna in spring water for 19¢. There may not always be a coupon for a product you want or need, but if you already shop at the Category #1 store once a week, coupons can provide additional value to your shopping cart with very little additional effort and expense.

# Captain Dad's Sea Chicken Flapjacks

Two 5-ounce cans of tuna in water
6 pieces whole wheat or multigrain
   bread, shredded
½ onion, diced
2 stalks celery
2 tablespoons olive or vegetable oil

2 pinches pepper
1 pinch salt
¼ cup water
4 tablespoons mayonnaise
2 tablespoons pickle relish
1 lemon, sliced

In a large mixing bowl, combine two 5-ounce cans of tuna in water, water included, 6 pieces of bread, ½ diced onion, 2 stalks of celery, 1 tablespoon of oil, 1 of pinch pepper, 1 pinch of salt, and ¼ cup of water. Mix. Depending on the amount of water in the tuna can, add additional water to create a pasty consistency. Place a frying pan on medium heat and add 1 tablespoon of oil. When the pan is hot, spoon 6 to 8 medium pancakes onto the pan, flatten with a fork or spatula and cook each side for 3 to 5 minutes or until desired browning is achieved. Combine 4 tablespoons of mayonnaise, 2 tablespoons of relish, and 1 pinch of pepper. As a garnish, add lemon slices to each plate. Preparation time is 20 to 25 minutes, and makes a somewhat unconventional, high-protein, low-fat snack for Captain Dad and his maties.

As a member of your Category #1 shopper rewards program and armed with loss-leader coupons, you're ready to shop. Given certain information, shopping on the same day of the week is a good idea for a couple of reasons. First, creating a routine for activities, like grocery shopping, may open up opportunities for efficiency.

A case in point is the Category #1 store's "senior discount day." Senior shoppers are a valuable commodity for Category #1 stores because, it seems, senior shoppers are consistent shoppers, but are also often price-sensitive. As such, Category #1 stores sometimes specify a day during the week on which special prices on certain products are offered in addition to other senior discounts, but those product discounts are also available to other shoppers. Moreover, the weekly loss-leader coupons may also coincide with senior discount day. In short, the day seniors shop is probably a pretty good day for anyone else to shop, too!

Although it may seem as unnatural to a single father as a left-handed shortstop, I recommend a shopping list, which will help insure that you bring home everything you need and nothing you don't. Even so, a list can still provide a little room for shopping autonomy. Hopefully, fruit is on the list. Within the context of "fruit," you can choose a few items which are on sale for shoppers with a rewards card. Based on seasonal factors, various exotic fruits may be specially priced. Buy pineapples, mangos, or watermelon for variety when the Category #1 store offers a good value!

Even within a single kind of fruit, for example, choose from a selection of items based on seasonally opportune pricing. Category #1 stores usually carry a dozen or more variety of apples, including Jazz, Pink Lady, Macintosh, Red Delicious, Golden Delicious, Honey Crisp, Jonagold, and Macoun, among others. Again, for various reasons, one or two types of apples may be deeply discounted, so stock up. Apples will usually last a couple of weeks in the refrigerator.

Shopping for fruit underscores the benefit of replacing traditional snack foods, like chips and pretzels, with fruits, but the game plan also works with fresh and frozen vegetables, meats, pastas, breads, and dairy. Although your own family's shopping list may vary based on geographic factors, personal taste, and brand preference, I recommend your Category #1 grocery store list include such items as:

- **Fresh fruits:** apples, oranges, bananas, seasonal items

- **Fresh vegetables:** lettuce, carrots, celery, seasonal items

- **Meats:** chicken, fish, beef, pork, or mutton; lunch meats

- **Canned goods:** soup, vegetables

- **Pasta:** whole wheat pastas

- **Breads:** whole wheat bread, bagels

- **Baking items:** whole wheat flour, soy flour, baking powder, artificial sweetener

- **Frozen foods:** vegetables, fruit

- **Dairy:** sliced cheese, shredded cheese, yogurt, sugar-free ice cream, butter

- **Special items:** soy milk, organic cow's milk

- **Miscellaneous** - dried fruit, nuts, soy nuts, granola bars, fruit cups

# Papito's Quesadillas con Pollo y Naranjas

4 flour tortillas

2 cups shredded cheddar cheese

8 ounces shredded chicken

2 pats butter

2 oranges

Heat a large pan to medium to medium-high heat. Melt 1 pat of butter in the pan. Add ½ cup of shredded cheddar cheese and 2 ounces of shredded chicken (most likely left over from the previous night's dinner), on each of the four tortillas. Fold in half and cook for about 2 minutes, two at a time, in the pan. Flip. Slice each quesadilla with a pizza cutter into four pieces. Serve with peeled and sectioned oranges. Total preparation time is 10 to 15 minutes, and feeds one *caballero* and his three *ninos.*

Within Category #2 grocery stores, there are two subcategories, either of which can serve your purposes of convenience and budget. On one hand, there are warehouse clubs like BJ's, Costco, and Sam's Club, where shoppers pay an annual membership fee for the privilege to shop at the "club." The benefit of the warehouse club is the bulk purchase discount. A bulk purchase discount is useful if your family consumes a great deal of certain foods. For example, if you and your children love farina, then you can save several dollars by purchasing a six-month supply in the form of a jumbo Cream of Wheat four-pack. While dry goods and canned goods can be money-savers, the purchase of perishable items can put a dent in your budget if they're allowed to spoil before you consume them. In addition, the membership fee at warehouse clubs may not justify the savings. It will be incumbent on you, the single father, to determine if the ends justify the means.

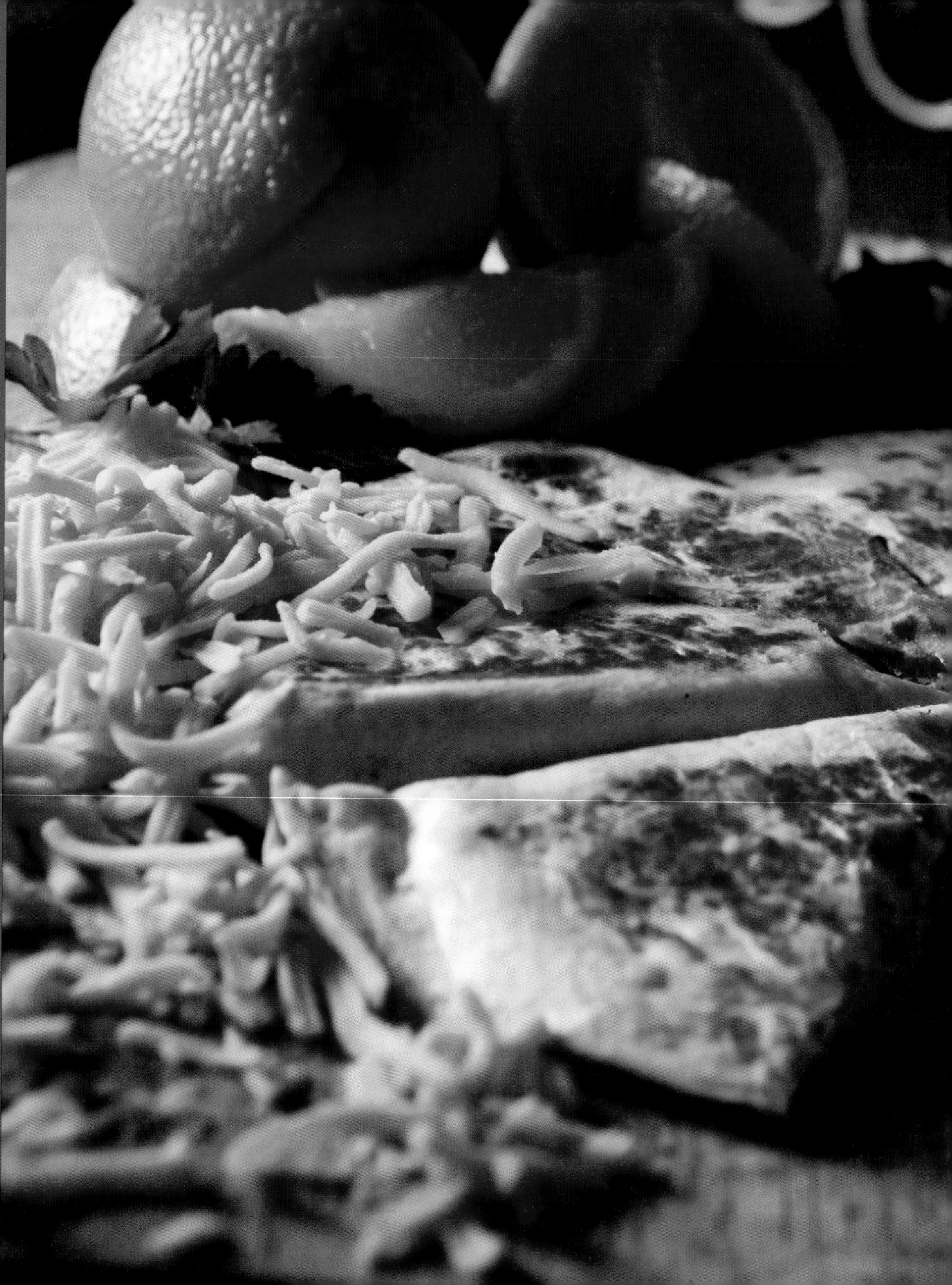

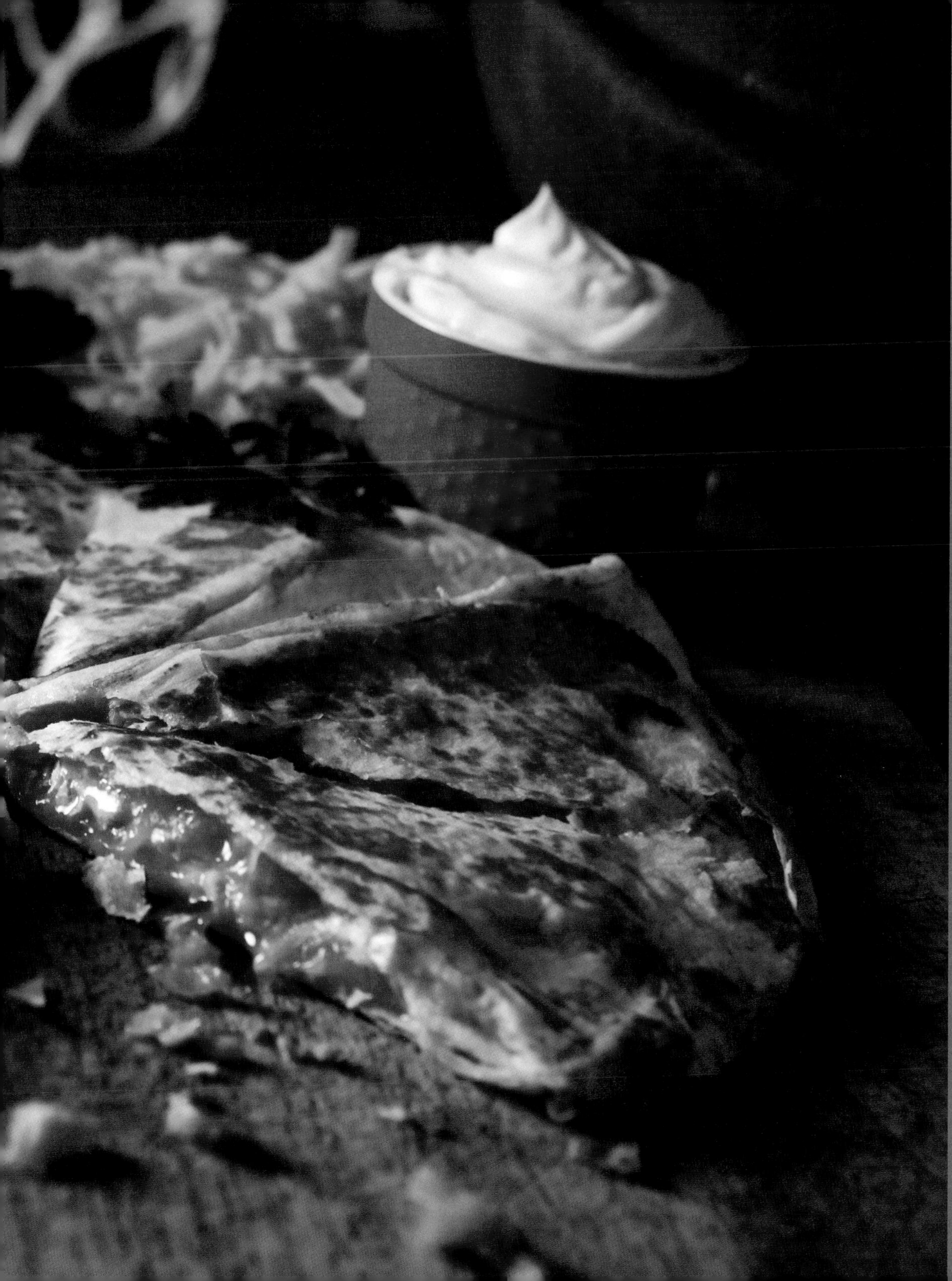

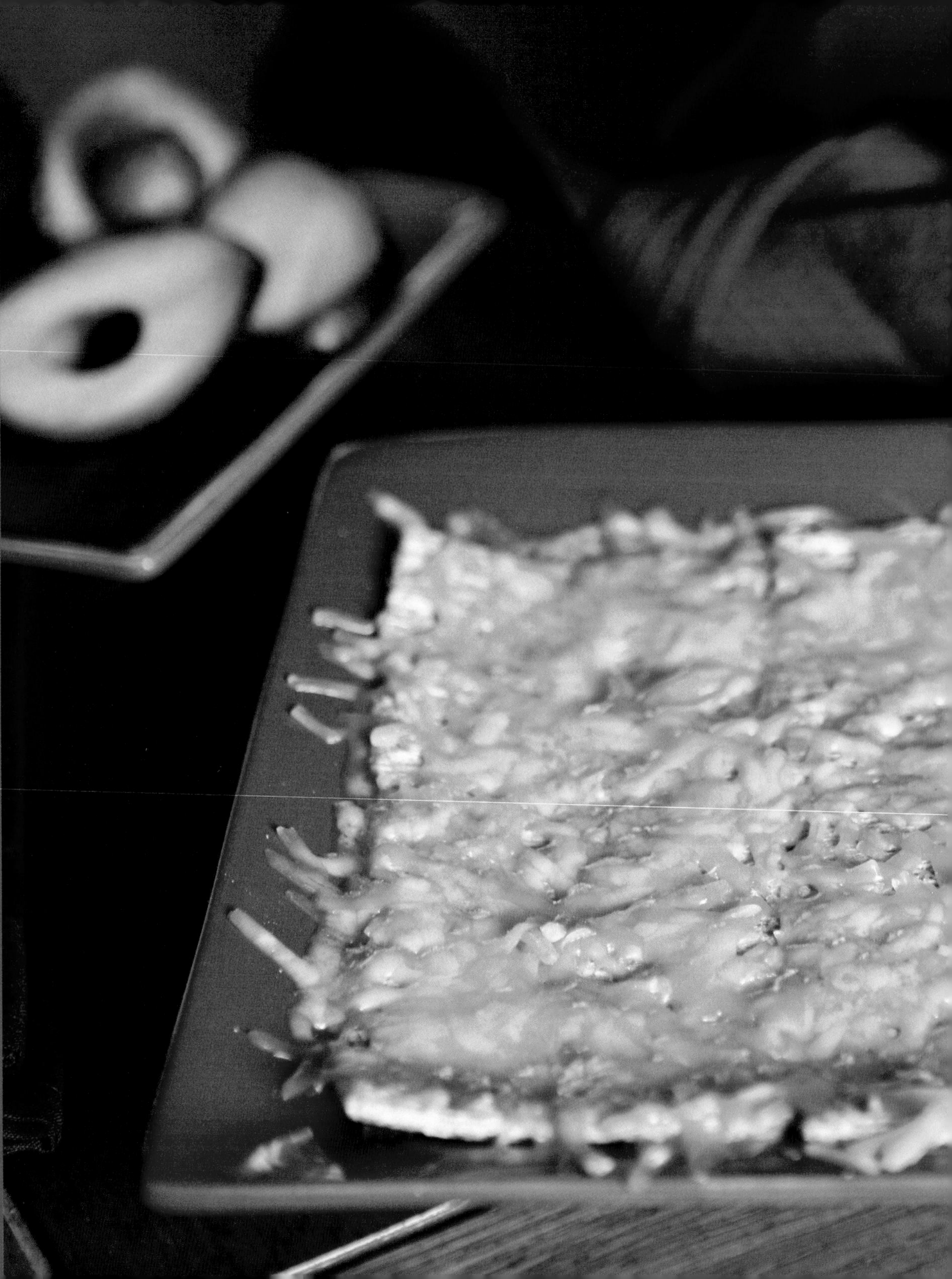

Discount grocery stores make up the balance of Category #2. While Aldi is perhaps the most recognizable brand among discount stores, independently owned and operated discount grocery stores have begun to spring up as well. One benefit that the discounter has over the warehouse club is that there's no annual membership. However, the quality and selection of the products is less consistent at the discount grocery store.

## Easy Cheesy Wheaty Crackers

20 to 24 woven wheat crackers
1 cup shredded cheddar cheese, or 4
   to 6 slices of deli cheddar cheese

1 avocado, sliced

Arrange the woven wheat crackers on a microwave-safe plate. Place 1 cup of shredded cheddar cheese or 4 to 6 slices of deli cheddar cheese on top of crackers. Place the plate in the microwave and cook on "high" for 60 to 75 seconds, or until the cheese is thoroughly melted. Garnish with sliced avocado. Total preparation time is 3 minutes or less, and provides a great, super-quick after-school snack for three young scholars. Dad can have some too, if he gets to it fast enough.

To the consumer's considerable benefit, discount grocers make special buys of manufacturer's and retail grocery store overstock of brand name items and supplier's seconds, and contract with various other growers and suppliers with a focus on price. In the case of overstocks, the product is often exactly the same brand as you'd find in a Category #1 store, but priced much lower. When the inventory of the special-buy item is gone, however, it's usually gone for good. On the other hand, the quality of supplier's seconds, especially fruits and vegetables, may suffer in comparison to those found in retail stores. One week, the oranges will be as good as those found at the retail grocery store, and another week, it may be the pineapples. In general, however, I tend to buy most of my produce and other fresh goods from Category #1 stores. And, finally, growers and suppliers that provide the balance of the discount store's stock often have a competitive advantage, like a local egg farm that doesn't have to include high transportation costs in its egg prices. I've found many of these generic items, including eggs, chicken, bacon, lunch meats, cheese, potatoes, rice, nuts, dried fruit, pasta, frozen fruit, condiments, and time-saving frozen entrees to be at least as good as those found at Category #1 stores.

Whether you choose a warehouse club or a discounter as your Category #2 store, I suggest that you make your selection based on both value and convenience. Once you've made your choice, make your visits to your Category #2 store as routine as your visits to your Category #1 store, with a slight departure. You'll typically make larger or bulk value purchases at the Category #2 store, so your visits will occur perhaps just every two to four weeks.

A number of factors will affect your Category #2 shopping list, but your list may include:

- Meats: chicken, fish, lean packaged cold cuts, bacon

- Canned Goods: soup, vegetables

- Cereals: farina, oatmeal

- Pasta: whole wheat pasta

- Staples: rice, potatoes

- Frozen foods: vegetables, fruit, breaded chicken, breaded fish, hamburger patties

- Dairy: sliced cheese, shredded cheese, yogurt, butter

- Miscellaneous: dried fruit, nuts, granola bars, fruit cups

Frozen meats are convenient when it comes to preparing healthy meals, but if you buy more fresh meat than you can eat within a few days after shopping, then invest in plenty of zipper-lock freezer bags. Then, take the meats from the "family-size" package, separate into single-meal-sized portions, and freeze. A few days later when you want catfish fillets, just pull a bag of three or four fillets out of the freezer in the morning and put it on a plate in the refrigerator to thaw in time for dinner!

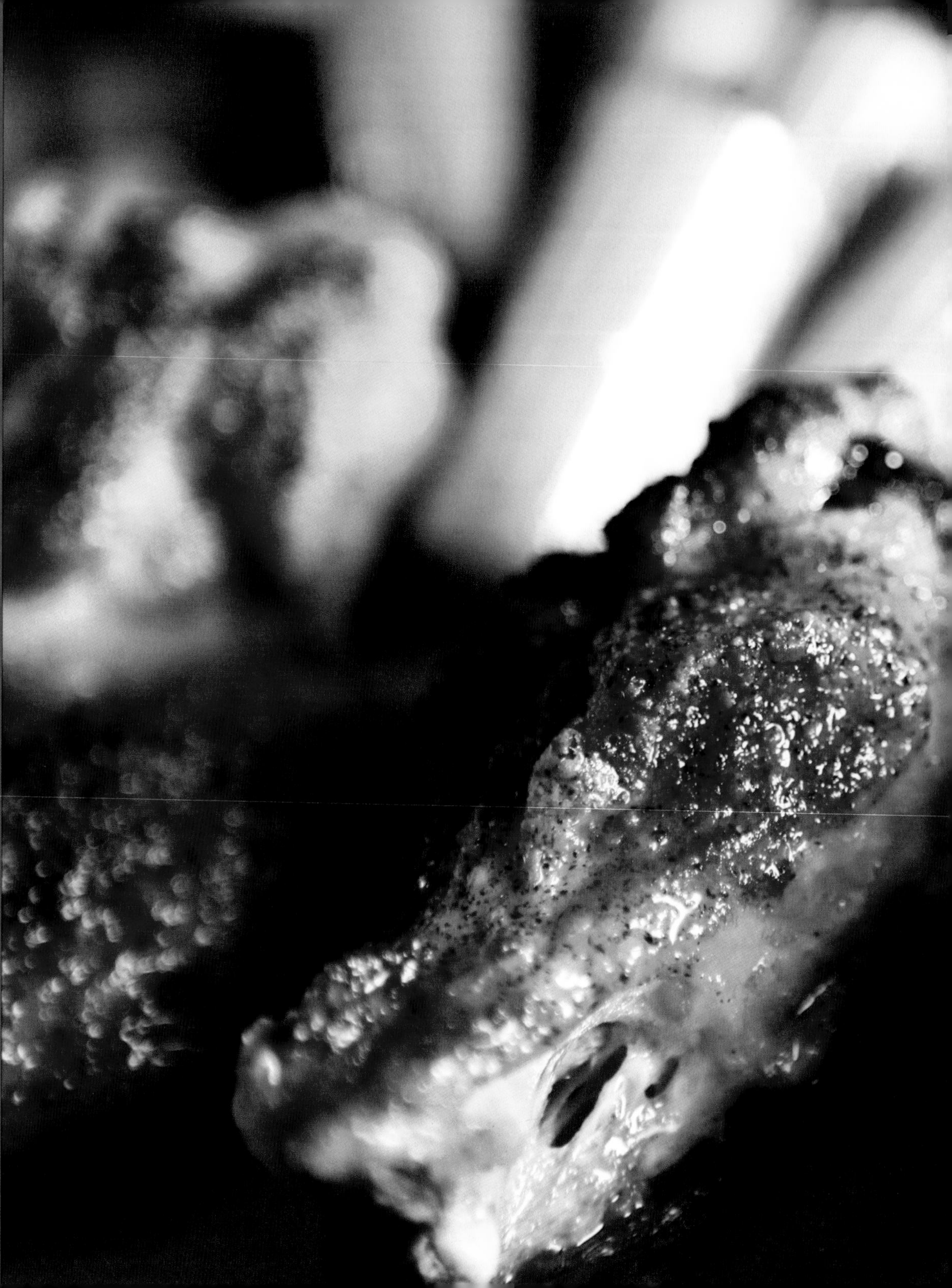

# The Old Man's Secret-Recipe Garlic Parmesan Chicken Wings

3 pounds frozen chicken wings

2 tablespoons butter

6 tablespoons parmesan cheese

2 teaspoons powdered garlic

1 teaspoon salt

1 teaspoon ground pepper

½ teaspoon paprika

4 ounces blue cheese or ranch dressing

6 sliced celery stalks

Preheat the oven to 375°. Coat the entire bottom and sides of a 9″ x 13″ baking pan with 2 tablespoons of butter. Sprinkle ¼ teaspoon of paprika, ½ teaspoon of ground pepper, ½ teaspoon of salt, 1 teaspoon of powdered garlic, and 3 tablespoons of ground or powdered parmesan cheese over the butter-coated pan. (Yes, right on the pan.) Empty 3 pounds of frozen chicken wings into the pan in a single layer. Sprinkle the remaining ¼ teaspoon of paprika, ½ teaspoon of ground pepper, ½ teaspoon of salt, 1 teaspoon of powdered garlic, and 3 tablespoons of ground or powdered parmesan cheese over chicken wings. Bake in a preheated oven for 60 minutes. Serve hot with 18 to 24 cut celery pieces and dressing on the side. The total preparation time is about 70 minutes, and is a filling snack for a single father's family of baseball fans while enjoying the playoffs!

It takes discipline to pass up the snack food aisle, and as far as I can tell, there's no real trick to doing it. You just have to do it. I realize that there are times when you and your kids crave the taste and texture of a sweet or a salty, crunchy snack. Before you reach for those bags of Cheese Doodles,

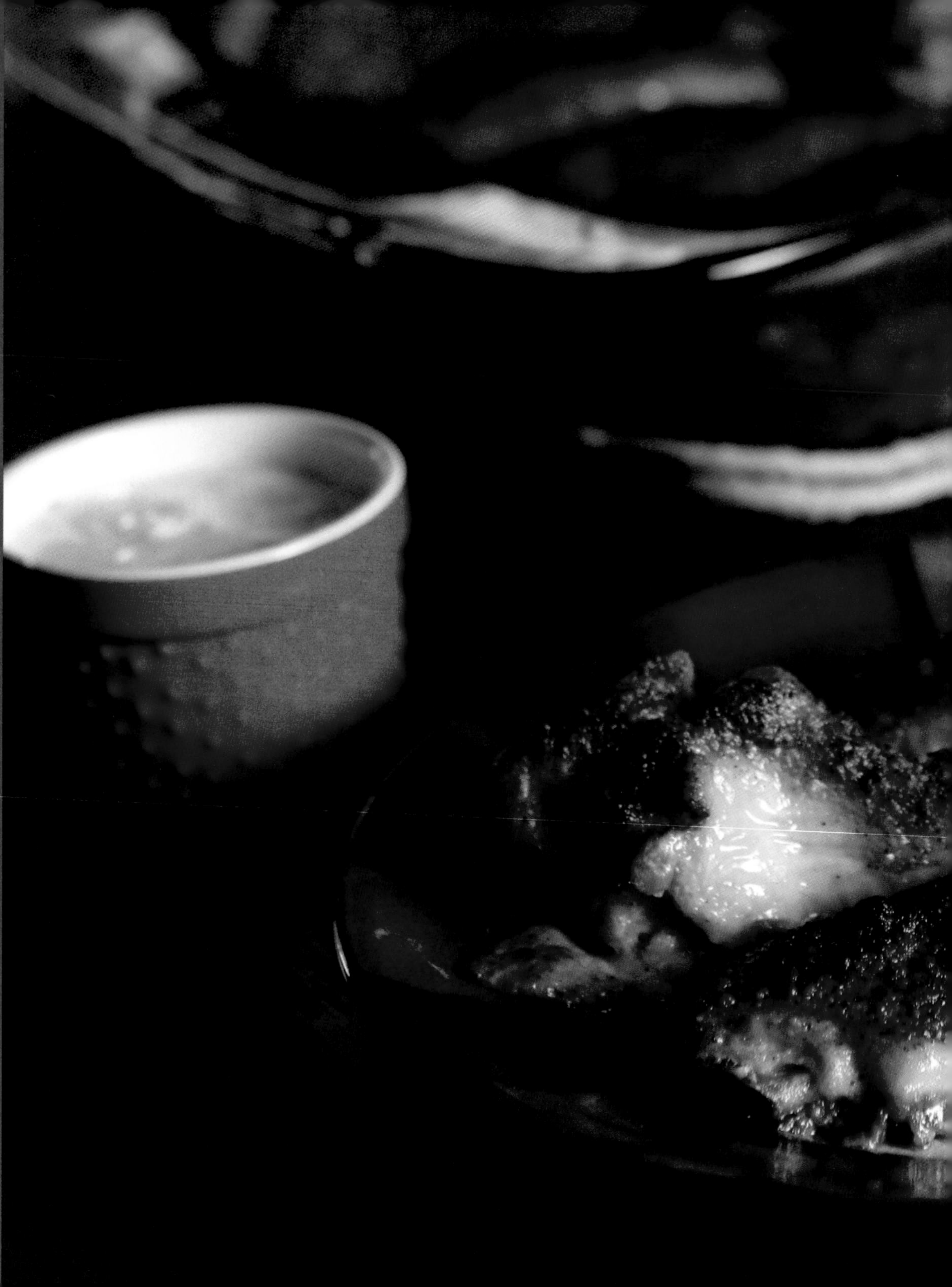

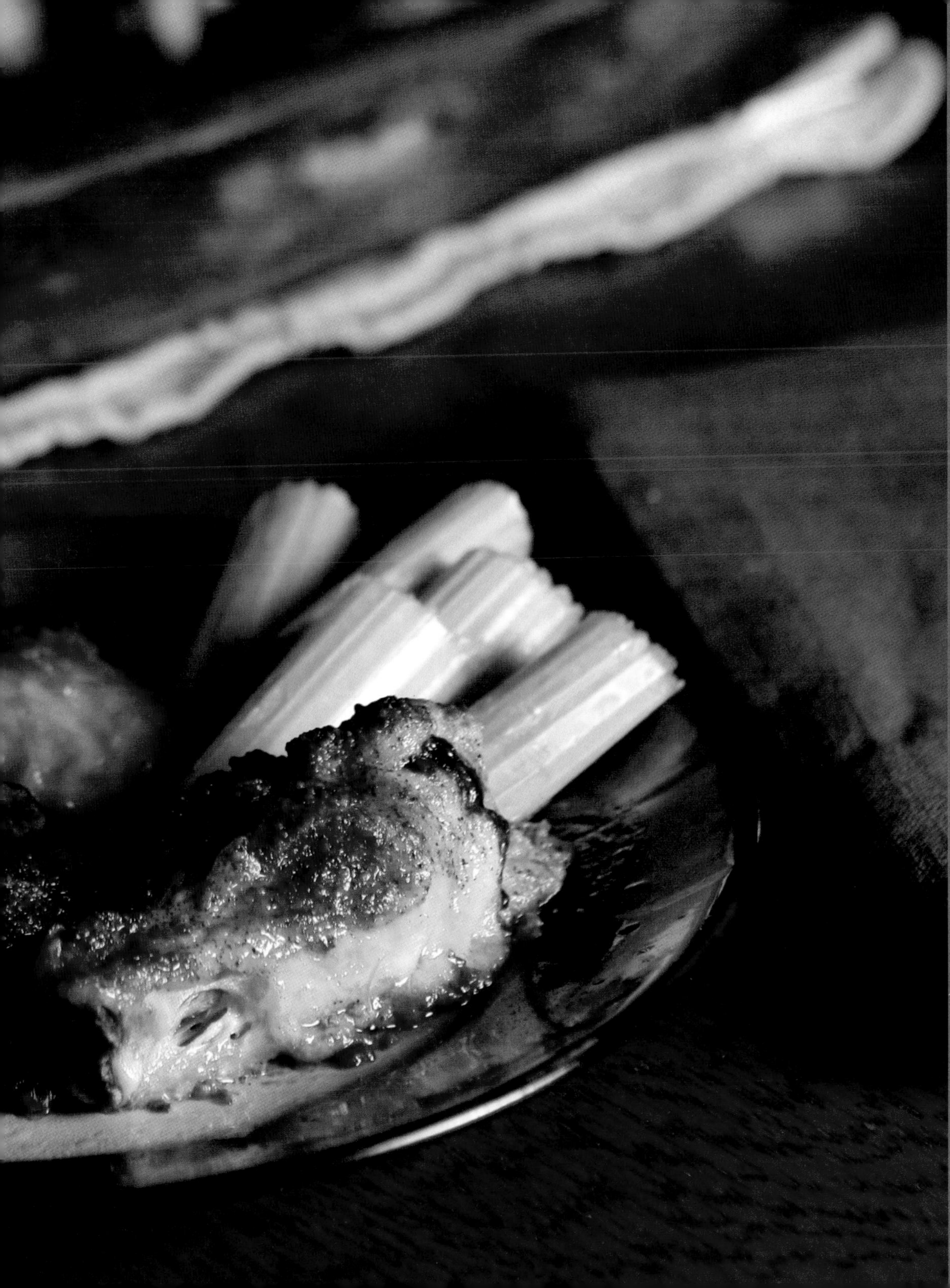

potato chips, and salty pretzels at the grocery store, though, recall The Single Father's Golden Rule #8: *If you don't bring junk food home in your grocery bags, you and your children won't eat it!*

I certainly don't advocate that you should stop snacking! Eating small snacks during the day can improve metabolism and moderate your appetite during the larger meals. So create a list of snack foods that will satisfy your hankering for something that's sweet or crunchy, and salty, while still offering some real nutritional benefits (even if you don't cut out all the processed sugar or sodium). For example, salty cashews are a vast improvement over salty potato chips. Substituting nuts for chips may not reduce sodium and the fat calories may be comparable, but you'll replace "easy" carbohydrates with protein. As a result, you may eat less and save calories to achieve the same degree of "snack satisfaction."

I encourage you to stock your snack bowl with nuts. If you have just a crunchy craving instead of a salty/crunchy craving, you can still "scratch your itch" with unsalted raw or roasted nuts and save the sodium!

Here are a few suggestions for snacks that help the single father comply with the goal of maintaining a healthy diet:

| | | |
|---|---|---|
| Almonds | Dried fruit, cranberries, | Nectarines |
| Apples | cherries, figs, raisins | Oranges |
| Bananas | Fruit cups | Peaches |
| Cashews | Granola bars | Pears |
| Cherries | Grapefruit | |
| Clementines | Grapes | |

To an extent, some of the fruits on the list, like clementines, nectarines, and peaches, are seasonal, but the seasonal variation in your snack bowl will help keep the offerings fresh and interesting.

## GOLDEN RULE #9:

### *Anyone can take from the snack bowl any time!*

Finally, the snack bowl is not a euphemism. Make a real snack bowl accessible to your entire family and stock it regularly with your healthy snacks. Apples, bananas, oranges, dried fruit, fruit cups, granola bars, nuts, and more should be ready for the taking, and create the foundation of The Single Father's Golden Rule #9: *Anyone can take from the snack bowl any time!*

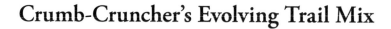

# Crumb-Cruncher's Evolving Trail Mix

One 8-ounce bag nuts, raw or
   roasted

One 8-ounce bag fruit, dried

One 8-ounce bag wasabi nuts

In a bowl, add nuts (almonds, cashews, pecans, etc.), dried fruit (blueberries, cherries, cranberries, raisins, etc.), and wasabi nuts. Mix with a spoon. Leave on the counter for general munching by dad and the kids. As stores diminish, replace with more of the same or some different items to mix it up!

Shopping the right way and replacing chips with healthy alternatives are essential steps in preventing you and your children from becoming "couch potatoes." Another is to limit opportunities to spend time on the couch.

Time is no friend of the single father. While television and other electronic devices serve valuable purposes ranging from providing entertainment to being important sources of information, those same devices can rob you of what little quality family time you have. During the school year, your children will most likely have to get out of bed between 5:30 a.m. and 7:00 a.m. to dress, eat, and catch the bus to school. Dismissal may be as early as 2:00 p.m. or as late as 4:00 p.m., after which there will need to be time for extracurricular activities, homework, and other interests, all of which are key components to fostering healthy, well-adjusted children. Frankly, television, game systems, social networking, and similar activities do not really fit into the weekday routine very well. Of course, it seems children develop an "acute loss of listening" when enmeshed in technology, which does no favors for the single father when it's time to eat, go to a practice, or go to bed.

*No television on weekdays* is The Single Father's Golden Rule #10, to which I add the corollary *Electronic devices may be used only on the first floor . . . and not in bedrooms.* Generally, enforcement of The Single Father's Golden Rule #10 is not terribly difficult considering I have only one television in the house. Keeping laptops out of the kids' bedrooms not only allows me to assist in varying degrees with schoolwork, but it also helps me to ensure that my little Internet surfers aren't being circled by cyber-sharks.

By eliminating television and controlling the use of electronics, I've made a few interesting discoveries, at least about my children. First, my kids are better listeners. I'm not sure whether reduced exposure to poorly behaving adolescents in television dramas is the reason, but cooperation improves.

## GOLDEN RULE #10:

*No television on weekdays*
*Electronic devices may be used only on the first floor . . .*
*and not in bedrooms.*

Second, academic performance has been consistently good. There are certainly a number of constants and variables that affect performance in school, but providing a distraction-free environment in which to do homework certainly does not hurt. Finally, when my kids have finished their homework and don't have any place else they need to be, they generally find relatively productive uses for their time. For my older kids, that use of time generally involves reading, and for my younger child, he plays with a toy, organizes his baseball card collection, or goes outside to play in the backyard.

Yes, there is a place and time for television and electronics. On the weekends, I am quite a bit more permissive when it comes to letting the kids "plug in" to "unplug" a little. Often, on Friday or Saturday night, we watch a movie as a family, on Saturday or Sunday afternoon, my son and I may watch a baseball or football game, and the girls will catch up with a couple of their favorite reality television or other shows that they'd programmed the DVR to record for them. When we do watch a movie, a ball game, or a reality TV show, I don't even mind so much when they sit down on the couch and snack on a sliced apple with peanut butter or hazelnut spread, a bowl of trail mix, or maybe even a few chicken wings!

# THE CLOSER
## DINNER

## Pop's Pesto Pasta with Broccoli

1 pound whole wheat pasta

1 tablespoon salt

3 cups broccoli

½ cup extra virgin olive oil

3 garlic cloves, diced

1 cup whole basil leaves or 1/3 cup
shredded basil leaves

¼ cup grated parmesan cheese

Fill a large cooking pot with 10 to 12 cups of water and 1 tablespoon of salt. Bring to a boil, and add 1 pound of whole wheat pasta. Follow the directions on the pasta package, or cook 5 to 10 minutes to desired softness. Drain the pasta.

At the same time, add a small amount of water to a saucepan, bring to a boil, reduce heat to low or medium-low, and add 3 cups of broccoli and cook approximately 10 minutes. Or place 3 cups of broccoli in a microwave-safe bowl, microwave on a high setting for 2 to 2½ minutes, then stir, and microwave for another 2 to 2½ minutes. Drain the broccoli.

In another saucepan, add ½ cup of extra virgin olive oil, 3 diced garlic cloves, shredded basil leaves, ¼ cup of parmesan cheese, and heat on medium-low for about 5 minutes.

In a large serving bowl, combine pasta, broccoli, and pesto sauce, and toss

until well mixed. The preparation time is approximately 20 minutes, and provides a tasty, balanced, and filling dinner for pop and three little peeps. (For variety, substitute peas or spinach for broccoli.)

A month before my employer "downsized" me (after moving my family and me from Saratoga Springs to Warwick, New York), and about three months before we learned Lori had cancer, we enrolled my two daughters in a nearby Taekwondo program.

At the first annual physical I had after Lori's diagnosis, my triglyceride and cholesterol levels exceeded the high end of normal for the first time.

I don't know whether the stress of my family's new reality resulted in a less healthy diet or whether it led directly to a change in my body chemistry, but the fact remained that I wasn't as healthy as I had been. I don't remember if it was a conscious decision to improve my health or if I just sought a stress reliever, but I soon began to practice martial arts with my daughters. Lori planned to join us after our son was born and after the cancer was in remission.

The martial arts school where we trained had two classes a week specifically designed for families. During those classes, the girls took a lot of pleasure in their relative "expert" status as compared with their "novice" dad, and neither ever missed the chance to coach me along. For my part, I treasured the opportunity to actually participate in the same activity with my kids, and, as a fringe benefit, I got great, tension-relieving exercise.

*When they start the game, they don't yell, "Work ball." They say, "Play ball."*
—Willie Stargell

We continued to make time for our family classes twice a week during the time when Lori received treatment, when our son was born, and as she battled her illness. Even when circumstances required me to spend more time at the hospital, there was never a shortage of great neighbors and good friends who helped us make sure the girls maintained their schedule at the school.

Lori was never able to practice martial arts with her family. However, martial arts not only became a fundamental part of our routine, but it also gave me both a regular outlet for my stress and something I've been able to maintain in common with my children. Upwards of a decade after the little six-year-old and four-year-old girls started taking martial arts classes, both are beautiful, confident, first-degree black belts. Now, their brother is almost one, too!

# Grilled Pork Chops, Cheddar-Garlic Mashed Potatoes, and Pan-Fried Brussels Sprouts

**Pork Chops**

3 to 4 pork chops

¼ teaspoon salt

¼ teaspoon pepper

1 clove garlic or 1 teaspoon garlic powder

½ teaspoon dried or fresh parsley, shredded

**Potatoes**

4 to 6 potatoes, washed, skin-on, and quartered

1 cup milk

4 ounces butter

3 cloves crushed garlic or 1 tablespoon garlic powder

1 cup shredded cheddar cheese

½ teaspoon salt

**Brussels sprouts**

12 ounces fresh or frozen brussels sprouts, thawed

1 tablespoon butter

½ teaspoon salt

103

Rub or spread ¼ teaspoon of salt, ¼ teaspoon of pepper, 1 clove of garlic (or 1 teaspoon of garlic powder), and ½ teaspoon of dried or fresh shredded parsley evenly among the pork chops. Grill on medium or medium-high heat for 6 to 10 minutes, depending on the grill; turn, and grill for another 6 to 10 minutes.

In a large cooking pot, bring the water to a boil, add 4 to 6 quartered potatoes, and cook for approximately 15 minutes or until the potatoes are tender. Drain water, and place the cooked potatoes in a large serving bowl. Add 4 ounces of butter, 3 cloves of crushed garlic or 1 tablespoon of garlic powder, 1 cup of shredded cheddar cheese, ½ teaspoon of salt, and mash together. Add milk to achieve the desired consistency.

In a medium or large frying pan, combine 1 tablespoon of butter, ½ teaspoon of salt, 12 ounces of brussels sprouts (thawed, if frozen), and sauté on low or medium-low heat for about 15 minutes.

The preparation time for this recipe is 30 to 40 minutes, depending on multitasking skills, and yields ample leftovers after one single father and his three children have finished.

Practicing Taekwondo, or more accurately, *continuing* to practice Taekwondo, has helped me to touch all bases when it comes to creating a recipe for success for me and for my family. First, the practice of martial arts was an activity in which my children were involved *before* we became a single-father family. Since the practice of martial arts was an activity we continued to do *after* we became a single-father family, Taekwondo helped to create a sense of familiarity and safety for my children and has been a symbol of our commitment to persevere in the face of adversity. Second, we continue to attend classes as a family, including my son once he was old enough. Taekwondo is a shared interest, and, by definition, a common bond. As such, it provides me with a mutual interest with which to lead off conversation as my children grow up and face the challenges of adolescence and young adulthood. Third, the classes we attend three days each week, on average, are outlets for stress and opportunities to burn calories. The exercise, added to a healthy diet, has helped to create healthier children and a healthier dad. (In my case, I've lost almost an eighth of my body weight and have kept it off!) Finally, the mental and physical mastery of a martial art is very practical. While the mental aspect of a martial art improves concentration, patience, and self-control, the physical piece may also be useful if a person finds himself in an unexpectedly difficult situation. The latter may be of particular benefit for a high school girl on a date or a college woman living on her own.

It just happened that my children practiced martial arts when our family crisis surfaced. There is nothing magical about Taekwondo, except for the fact that my children and I enjoy it. For any single father, the activities that maintain your family's routine, help you to connect with your children, and contribute to your emotional and physical health are a matter of personal preference. The important lesson happens to be The Single Father's Golden Rule #11: *Identify at least one activity that your family enjoys and is one in which you can regularly participate together.*

While I encourage the single father to look at the activities in which you and your children may already be involved, here are a few suggestions, based, of course, on your age, your children's ages, and your personal interests, if you happen to be starting from scratch:

| | | |
|---|---|---|
| Canoeing | Hunting | Shooting |
| Coaching youth | Fishing | (National Rifle |
| sports | Hiking | Association, etc.) |
| Cycling | Running | Swimming |
| Gardening | Sailing | Tennis |
| (Future Farmers of | Scouting | |
| America, 4H, etc.) | (Boy Scouts, Girl | |
| Golf | Scouts, etc.) | |

Children of the single father may continue to have other interests in which the single father cannot actually participate, like varsity football or drama club. Obviously, children should be allowed to participate and develop their potential in these activities, but the activities both you and your children can enjoy throughout your lifetimes should be developed in parallel. After your children have grown, those activities may be rediscovered in a different context years in the future.

## GOLDEN RULE #11:

*Identify at least one activity that your family enjoys and is one in which you can regularly participate together.*

Regardless of the activity you choose, or, as the case may be, the activity that chooses you, stick with it! Participate regularly. By doing so, you'll feel better, you'll learn something, and you'll connect with your children. Equally important, your children will connect with you!

*Baseball is the only place in life where a sacrifice is really appreciated.*
—**Author unknown**

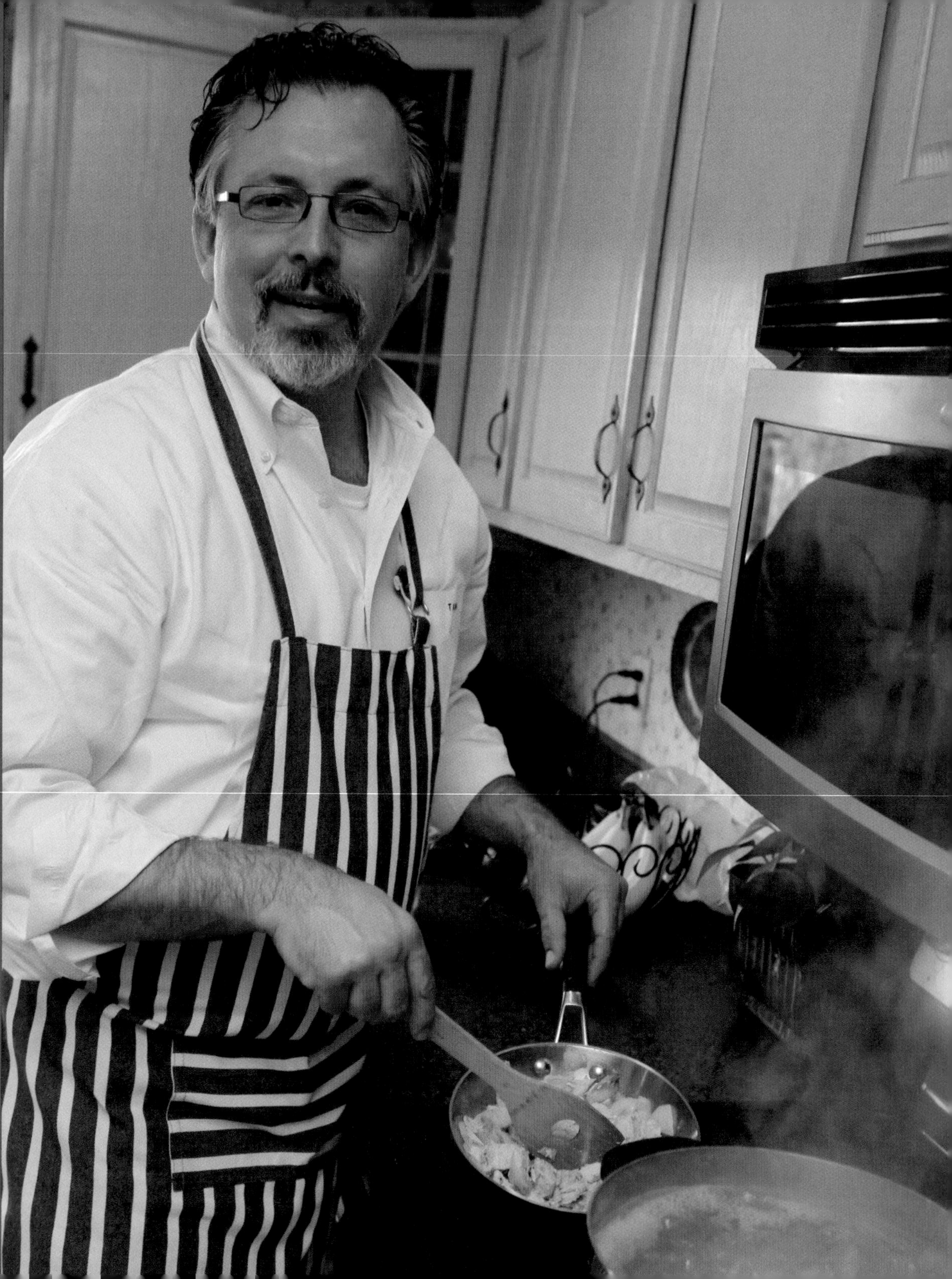

# Dad's Irish-Up Shepherd's Pie

12 ounces meat (leftover beef, chicken, pork, turkey, or ground beef or turkey)

12 to 16 ounces frozen corn kernels, peas, or carrots, thawed and drained

4 cups Cheddar-Garlic Mashed Potatoes (see Grilled Pork Chops, Cheddar-Garlic Mashed Potatoes, and Pan-Fried Brussels Sprouts recipe)

½ cup diced onion

⅓ cup shredded cheddar cheese

¼ teaspoon salt

¼ teaspoon pepper

2 ready-made, packaged pie shells

Preheat the oven to 375°. In a large pie pan, place one pie shell. Reheat (or brown) meat in a pan with salt, pepper, and diced onions, drain, and spoon into the bottom of pie shell. Add thawed, drained vegetables over the meat. Sprinkle shredded cheddar cheese over the vegetables. Add Cheddar-Garlic Mashed Potatoes over the shredded cheddar. Place the second pie shell over the potatoes, crimp the edges, and make small cuts with a knife in the top crust to vent. Bake for 40 minutes until the crust is golden brown. Remove from the oven, let cool for 10 minutes, and serve. Feeds a single-father family of four, and there may even be enough left for a snack or to be included in somebody's lunch box the next day!

Personally, I'm a dog person. Back in the day when I was a kid, people didn't worry so much about off-leash dogs, and the only pit bull terrier I'd ever seen was Petey from the reruns of *The Little Rascals*. My family had a great, mild-tempered, somewhat-overweight beagle named Barney. In St. Charles

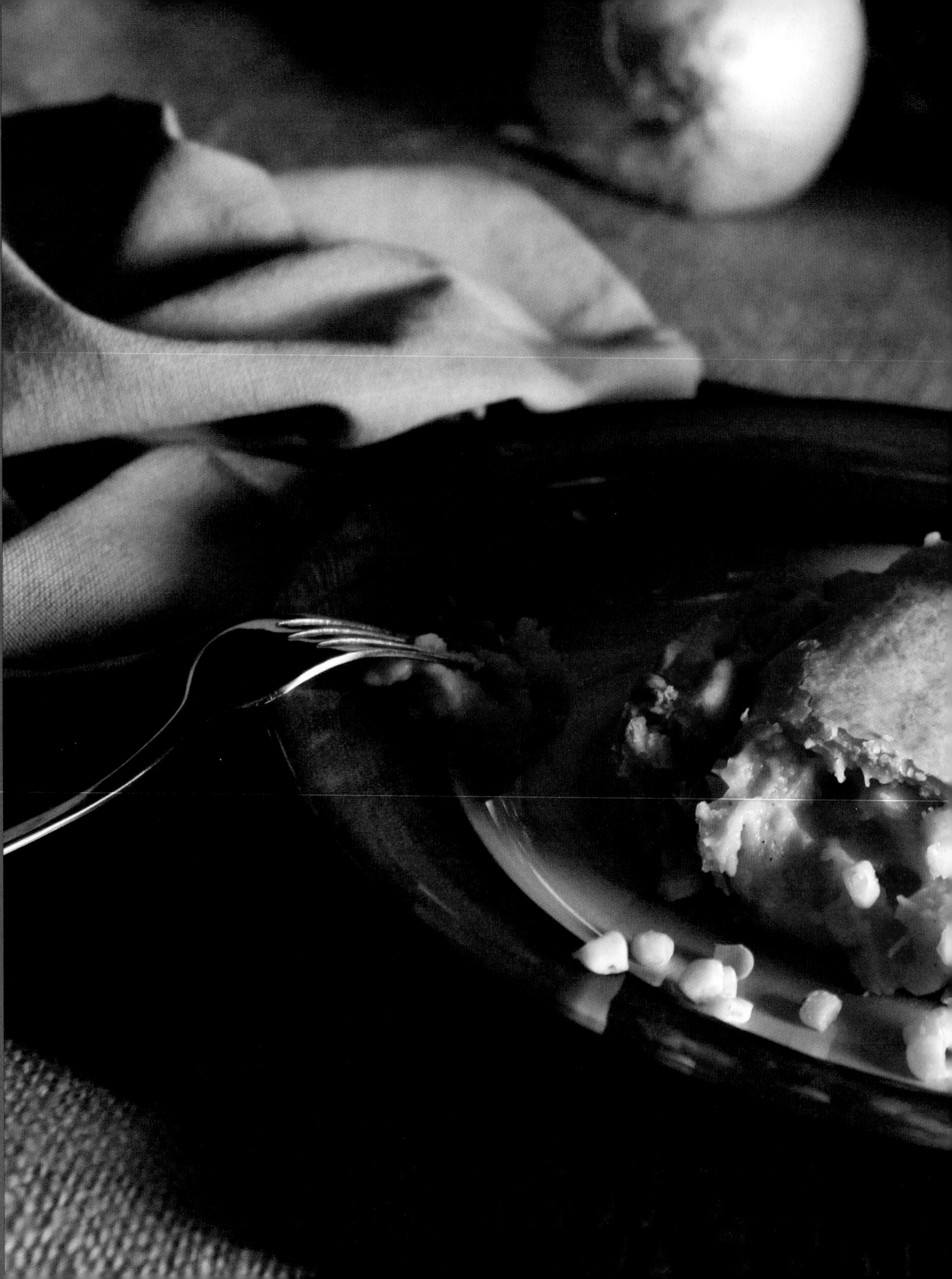

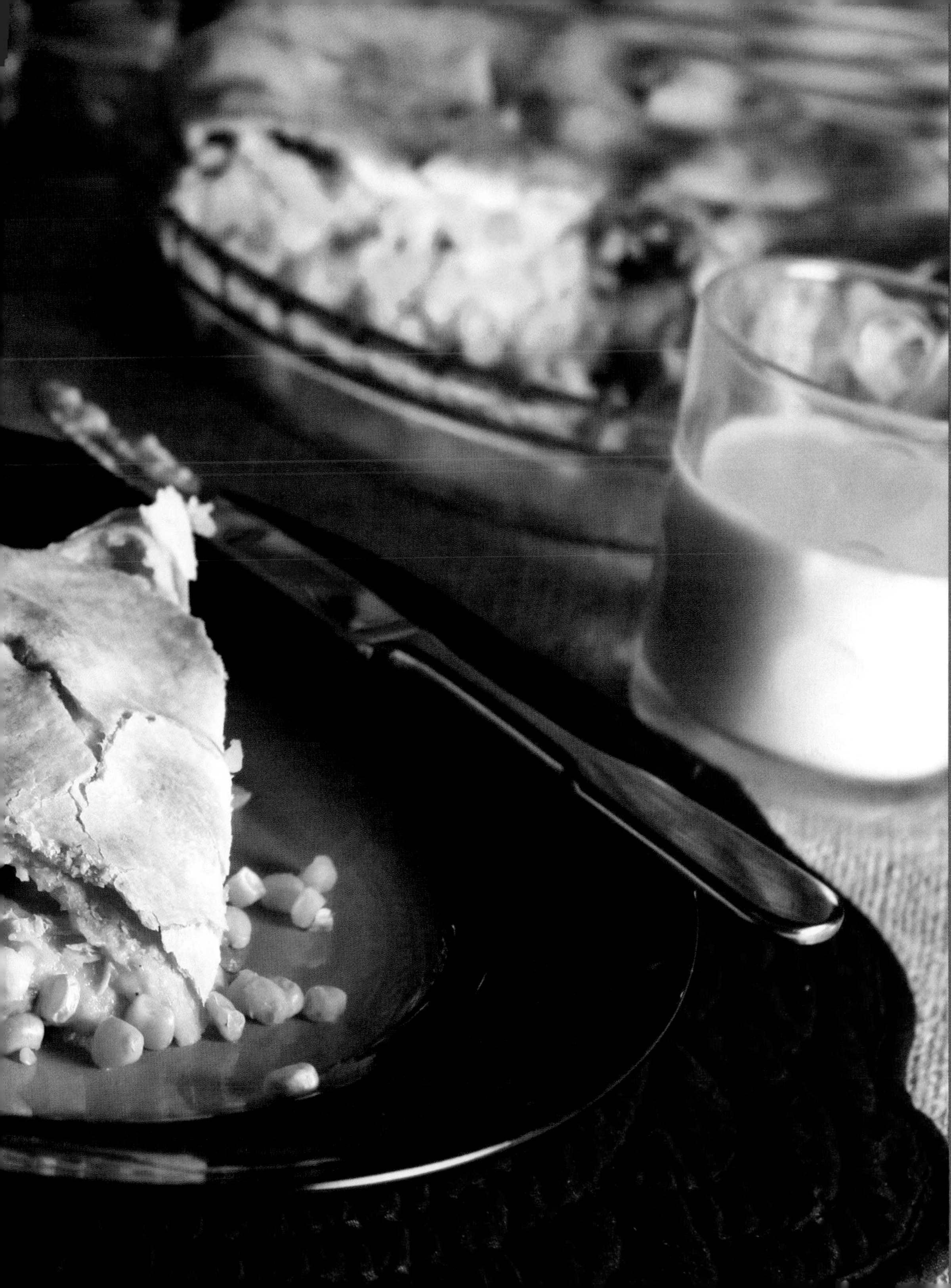

County, Missouri, which at the time was truly rural Missouri, Barney blended in with all of the farm dogs that ran the woods and cornfields that bounded the development where I lived. After the adventures with his fellow hounds ended each day, he'd usually come home for a meal of canned dog food, which he often ate right off the ground, and serve as the sentry at our 1960s-era ranch-style home. My experience with Barney is, in large part, the reason I am comfortable now with dogs and with all animals, domestic and wild.

As one-half of a young married couple who, twenty years later, had yet to start a family, I really wanted a dog. In my mind's eye, our dog would be our faithful companion and join my wife and me on our adventures, which, I imagined, could include anything from hikes through the swampy New England wilderness to our trips to the hardware store. So, on a warm, spring evening, the two of us set off to a small coastal village in Connecticut to see a backyard breeder who'd advertised German shepherd puppies for sale. We gave the owners a cash deposit, and returned a few weeks later to bring home our new puppy, which we named Mozart.

In all, our experience with dog ownership drew my wife and me closer together. Mozart was truly our faithful companion at farmers markets, county fairs, and vacations, and he was, almost without exception, a perfect gentleman. He was the reason I started a habit of walking two miles every morning before I went to work. On at least one occasion, Mozart gave a prowler enough of a reason to reconsider our house as a target for his nefarious intents. He was time consuming and often frustrating, but my fondness for Mozart was simply a reflection of the affection I had for Lori and the life we were creating together.

Mozart had departed for Doggie Heaven several years before single fatherhood was thrust upon me. A household cat, Bootsie, had been our family pet for a couple of years. For the most part, a second-grader and a kindergartener aren't much help with the responsibilities associated with pet ownership. At the same time, I had my hands full with helping two little girls process the loss of their mother, performing the necessary duties to get them to and from school and activities every day, while at the same time feeding, bathing, changing diapers, and providing a nurturing environment for a seven-month-old boy. Frankly, the last thing I needed to worry about was kitty litter, food, fleas, and veterinarian visits. However, I recalled my childhood connection with Barney, and imagined how I would have felt if Barney would have been taken away from me under the best of circumstances! For a lot of reasons, not the least of which was my commitment to provide an environment based on routine and tradition and to create a "safe" place where my children could process their emotions, Bootsie obviously stayed.

Some time after the kids lost their mother, in an obvious moment of weakness, I made what I believe was one of the more grievous mistakes that I've made as a single father: I adopted not just one new pet kitten; I got two.

My intentions were good. Simply, I was proud of my girls for the way they had dealt with the dramatic changes in their lives, whether they actually knew they were doing it or

*Baseball is like a poker game. Nobody wants to quit when he's losing; nobody wants you to quit when you're ahead.*
—Jackie Robinson

not. I wanted to reward them, which was a small way of reinforcing their behavior. I quickly learned I had made a colossal error in my judgment.

I'm a sucker for cute, and I adopted a couple of cute, cuddly siblings from the same litter at an extremely well-run Humane Society in Warwick, New York. The staff at the Warwick Humane Society has the practice of naming all the animals that reside within its walls, and mine had been christened "Clinton" and "Kennedy."

In our suburban, center-hall colonial home, all of the bedrooms were upstairs. The master bedroom was directly adjacent to the stairs. After I'd become a single father, I'd gotten into the habit of sleeping with my door open, so I could more easily hear the kids if they needed anything, and I could guard against roamers or sleepwalkers. The kids already preferred to keep their door open at night.

Clinton and Kennedy were fun and friendly during the day. When the girls were home, they'd play and frolic together. While just the baby and I were home, they'd mostly sleep. They'd sleep, of course, because they needed their energy to ransack the house at night.

After the sun when down, the kittens would wrestle and spar like Earl Weaver and the American League umpires. The frolicsome growls were often accompanied by rattling curio cabinets or the occasionally falling salt shaker. When Clinton and Kennedy grew weary of playing alone, they'd attempt to enlist me or one of the kids by literally jumping on our heads. The kids and I were losing sleep, which, in turn, produced a number of other exasperating results.

The girls were tired, so they were crabby and uncooperative, which tried my own sleep-deprived, shortened fuse. Getting ready for school, homework, and participation in our regular extracurricular activities all became more challenging, and I still needed to be the primary caregiver for a toddler. Of course, the additional responsibilities of pet care remained as well. The litter needed cleaning two or three times more often with three cats —we still had Bootsie—than with one. Kittens are still on a learning curve when it comes to using the litter box, so there were also the slightly-more-than-occasional accident cleanups. Veterinary visits and repairing damages committed by our new housemates contributed to our collective energy drain. In spite of all this, the girls loved Clinton and Kennedy, and I was loathe to take the animals away.

First, I tried just closing our bedroom doors at night. I learned that the practices that children hold dear can be pretty interesting. Sleeping with an open door was one of those things. My son didn't seem to mind, but closing the girls' doors created anxiety and didn't help them sleep any better. Although sleeping with my door closed wasn't necessarily a problem for me, other than the fact I couldn't monitor with my sixth sense the kids sleeping and the stairs. However, my feline friends simply decided to hold their wrestling tournaments outside my door, against which the two regularly slammed their cuddly little bodies.

Then I moved the kittens to the basement at night so we could once again sleep with our bedroom doors open. This solution did help the girls, but did little to improve my lot. Like many homes with a center hallway design, the stairwells are stacked, one on top of the other. As such, I could still hear the siblings, this time crying for their freedom. In addition, cleanups in the basement, for some reason, increased rather than waned.

*There is one word in America that says it all, and that one word is, "You never know."*
—**Joaquin Andujar**

In the end the responsibilities associated with our new pets, specifically, *my* responsibilities associated with our new pets, became untenable after only a couple of months. During dinner one night, I explained to the kids the best I could that caring for Clinton and Kennedy was taking too much time and energy from caring for them. They, in turn, understood the best they could. Although they were a little sad, surprisingly, they agreed. I supposed my daughters didn't get more upset because they experienced their own frustrations with the "little presidents" and because they didn't completely bond with them.

In a relatively short time, I found a nice home and a family who had different circumstances than I did and who were better equipped to contend

## GOLDEN RULE #12:

*If you already have a family pet when you become a single father, keep it. If you don't already have a family pet when you become a single father, for the sake of your sanity, don't get one!*

with the two high-energy kittens. The kids came with me to meet the new owners, which I think helped them cope with this new change I'd created, and the emotional fallout, thankfully, was minimal.

This could have been a much bigger problem for the kids, and, by association, for me. An act that sprung from the best of intentions resulted in what could only be described as a detrimental experience. There may not be a better example of the aphorism (adapted from St. Bernard de Clairvaux's quote[19]) "The road to hell is paved with good intentions." This idea led directly to The Single Father's Golden Rule #12: *If you already have a family pet when you become a single father, keep it. If you don't already have a family pet when you become a single father, for the sake of your sanity, don't get one!*

# Dad's Super Salad with Grilled Chicken

1 head lettuce

1 pound grilled boneless chicken, cut into chunks

¼ teaspoon salt

¼ teaspoon pepper

1 apple, with the skin on, cut into chunks

1 cup salted or unsalted almonds or cashews

1 cup shredded cheddar cheese

½ cup dried blueberries, cherries, cranberries, or raisins

12 woven wheat crackers, crushed

Season raw chicken with salt and pepper and pan fry or grill on medium or medium-high heat for about 8 to 10 minutes on each side or until fully cooked, and cut into chunks. De-core the lettuce and peel off the outer leaf before tearing or cutting the leaves into small, salad-sized pieces. Add warm chicken chunks, apple chunks, almonds or cashews, cheddar cheese, dried fruit, and crushed woven wheat crackers. Toss. Serve with your favorite salad dressings. The total preparation time is roughly 20 to 25 minutes, and serves three healthy children and their dad, who doesn't mind a couple of cookies for dessert after this healthy meal!

Dad's Super Salad with Grilled Chicken is a great meal for a lot of reasons, not the least of which is the taste! Obviously, "eating your vegetables" is never a bad idea, and making a vegetable the foundation of a meal is nutritionally sound. The flavors and textures in a good salad provide not only a meal that satiates your hunger, but also one that provides a little of that emotionally satisfying comfort food experience as well.

While there is a benefit to reducing sodium, this is one of those times when I've been willing to trade the benefit of using unsalted nuts for the benefit of "scratching the snack itch." The salted nuts along with the woven wheat crackers in the salad provide both the salt and the crunch that taste buds crave, and they agreeably balance the soft and the sweet provided by the dried fruits. Then the apple and the cheese also counterbalance, offering a sweet-crunchy and a salty-soft taste, respectively. To add to the flavor extravaganza, the warm chicken complements the cold salad and apple and produces an entirely new dimension.

Nutritionally, Dad's Super Salad with Grilled Chicken supplies protein in three forms from the chicken, the nuts, and the cheese. All three are rich in minerals like iron and calcium, and mostly "good" fats. The apple, lettuce, and dried fruit contribute vitamins, including vitamins A and C, while all three plus the crushed woven wheat crackers supply ample fiber, which will help you feel fuller, longer!

In our family, schedules always seem the busiest during the last six weeks before the end of the calendar year, and during the last six weeks before the end of the school year. Given the choice between the two, I'm not sure which I'd prefer to navigate. Near the end of the calendar year, beginning around Thanksgiving, the days are packed with family gatherings, holiday shopping, office parties, school concerts and plays, the end of the fall athletic seasons, and religious observances. These activities are usually further complicated by the variety of nontraditional family situations a single father has to pilot, especially in the case of divorce. Then, because of the children, what used to have been the need to visit "both sides" of the family may double if both parents have romantic interests. On the other hand, Memorial Day travel and activities, end of school parties both at school and at friends' houses, summer athletic seasons, school field trips, and again, concerts and plays may trouble even the most experienced logistician. Fortunately, or unfortunately, we don't have a choice! The seasons arrive annually and without fail whether we want them to come or not.

What happens during those times when everyone's schedules are so busy that you haven't made it to the grocery store, but you still want to provide a sustaining and enjoyable meal for your family? Well, one option is to make do with the last items you happen to have in the pantry and freezer. (Doesn't it always seem like lima beans are the last to go?)

# "Dad's Helper" Turkey Burger Mac with Lima Beans

| | |
|---|---|
| 1 pound ground turkey burger | 1 tablespoon vegetable oil |
| 1 box macaroni and cheese | 1 tablespoon butter |
| 12 ounces lima beans, fresh | ½ teaspoon salt |
| or frozen | ¼ teaspoon pepper |

Over medium or medium-high heat, add 1 tablespoon of vegetable oil, 1 pound of ground turkey, ¼ teaspoon of salt, and ¼ teaspoon of pepper to a frying pan. Brown. Prepare macaroni and cheese according to the box instructions. Stir in browned ground turkey to the cooked macaroni and cheese. In a small saucepan, bring ½ cup of water, 1 tablespoon of butter, and ¼ teaspoon of salt to a boil. Reduce heat to simmer, and add 12 ounces of lima beans. Cook covered for about 10 minutes or until the beans are tender. The preparation time is about 15 to 20 minutes. Feeds a somewhat stressed-out single father and his three busy children, while allowing the Old Man to postpone his grocery shopping for one more day!

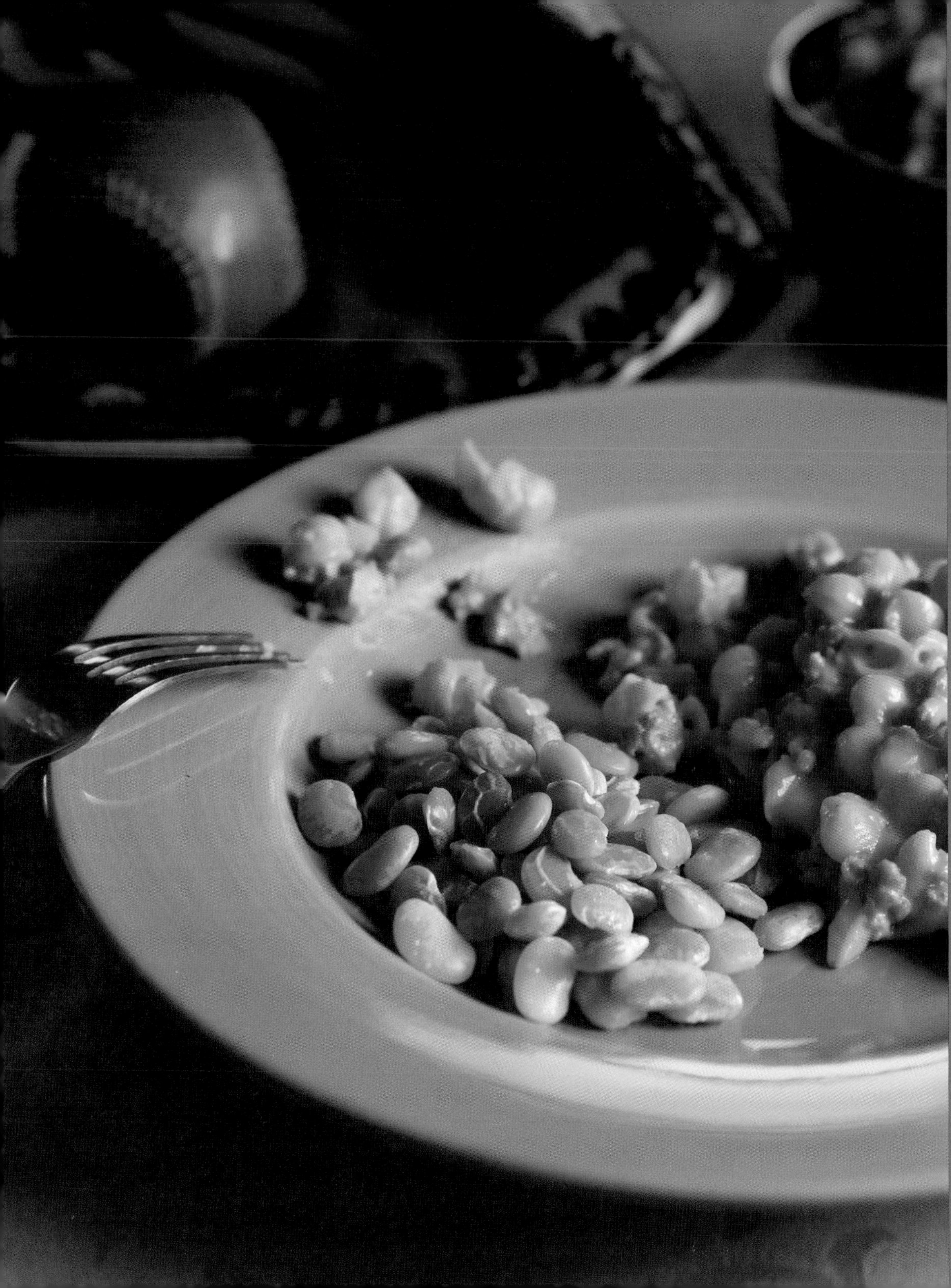

Again, I don't necessarily espouse "calorie counting." Rather, I just want to make balanced meals. However, to make a point, the total calorie count for this meal, based on the nutritional information on each of the packages, is only about 2,800 calories. About half come from the boxed macaroni and cheese, about 900 from the pound of turkey burger, and the remainder comes from lima beans, butter, and vegetable oil. Obviously, if divided equally among a family of four, the recipe results in about 700 calories per person, which is pretty reasonable for any meal that includes a box of mac 'n' cheese.

Of course, the other option is eating out.

# AWAY GAMES
## EATING OUT AND GOING OUT

In addition to nutrition, a fundamental theme throughout *The Single Father's Guide* is convenience. Time is as valuable a resource as you have, and if a single father will have any chance to enjoy a healthy, balanced life, you will have to utilize every resource at your disposal. Those resources do, in fact, consist of restaurants—even fast-food! Just like during the long baseball season, the focus is not as much on moderation as it is about simply making good decisions.

Hopefully, some of the suggestions I've given you and some ideas you've discovered independently have made you a better time manager. The little bits of time you've discovered as a by-product of the effective management of your schedule and your family's will have been invested in creating healthy meals and shared with your children in common interests. As a result, you're happier and healthier because you eat right and exercise and because your children are comfortable and happy in their routine, which also includes a good diet and physical activities.

At some point, the demands on your time—which will likely include your work, your children's schedules, and your personal life—simply prevent you from even getting home to make a meal. Then, you see a fast-food restaurant.

So, now you've created a healthy lifestyle, which has resulted in healthier children who perhaps don't need to go to the pediatrician as often as they otherwise might have; and chosen convenient places to get groceries, which reduces your driving time; You've participated with your children in interests and activities, which has reduced the demand on you to find additional avenues to relieve stress. As a result, you've discovered more time! So, now, you don't have to eat at fast-food restaurants as often as you used to.

This is a good thing, of course, because it's a game of inches. For example, assume you'd been in the habit of eating at a fast-food restaurant like Wendy's once a week. Your typical meal might have been a quarter-pound "Single" with cheese, medium French fries, and a medium Coca-Cola, which translates into 1,220 calories, 49 grams of fat, and 164 grams of carbohydrates![20] Just by substituting the Dad's Helper Turkey Burger Mac with Lima Beans recipe every other week, you'll save about 520 calories twenty-six times, or 13,520 calories in a year's time. For you, that's the equivalent of more than five days of the RDA for calories. For your kids, depending on age of course, it's more than a week's worth of calories!

> *No game in the world is as tidy and dramatically neat as baseball, with cause and effect, crime and punishment, motive and result, so cleanly defined.*
> —Paul Gallico

Fast-food establishments have so successfully proliferated, at least in part, because of their convenience. Most single fathers have probably already realized that there are times when you need that convenience. Still, there are ways to eat healthier when you do.

Let's start with that typical meal from Wendy's, a quarter-pound Single with cheese, medium French fries, and a medium Coca-Cola (see Table A).

While a properly prepared potato can add a healthy source of the energy you and your children need to hurtle through your daily activities, French fries, skinned, fried in oil, and heavily salted, offer little in the way of nutrition but a great deal in the form of empty calories and fat. In this meal, the fries contain roughly as many calories and fat grams as the burger, and about a third of the meal's carbohydrates.

Substitute apple slices for the fries, which not only significantly reduces calories, fat, and carbohydrates but also adds vitamins. making the calories "full" rather than "empty." (see Table B).

Table A.

| ITEM | CALORIES | FAT (G) | CARBOHYDRATE (G) |
|------|----------|---------|------------------|
| Quarter-pound Single w/cheese | 550 | 28 | 43 |
| Medium French fries | 420 | 21 | 55 |
| Medium Coca-Cola | 240 | 0 | 66 |
| Total | 1,210 | 49 | 164 |

Table B.

| ITEM | CALORIES | FAT (G) | CARBOHYDRATE (G) |
|------|----------|---------|------------------|
| Quarter-pound Single w/cheese | 550 | 28 | 43 |
| Apple slices | 40 | 0 | 9 |
| Medium Coca-Cola | 240 | 0 | 66 |
| Total | 830 | 28 | 118 |

Like just about all sugary drinks, soda is only calories and carbohydrates, which, if consumed, guzzle a person's available RDA calories, but provide no nutritional benefits. The Single Father's Golden Rule #13: *Replace sugary drinks, including soft drinks, fruit juices, and energy drinks with water or other no-sugar-added beverages.*

Swapping the Coca-Cola for a Nestea Unsweetened Iced Tea starts to become a healthy meal (see Table C).

While you're at it, why don't you go all the way? Making your entrée a salad rather than a burger not only moderates the calories, fat, and carbohydrates, but also provides 80 percent of the RDA for vitamin A and 70 percent for vitamin C (see Table D)!

## GOLDEN RULE #13:

*Replace sugary drinks, including soft drinks, fruit juices, and energy drinks with water or other no-sugar-added beverages.*

**Table C.**

| ITEM | CALORIES | FAT (G) | CARBOHYDRATE (G) |
|---|---|---|---|
| Quarter-pound Single w/cheese | 550 | 28 | 43 |
| Apple slices | 40 | 0 | 9 |
| Nestea Unsweetened Iced Tea | 0 | 0 | 0 |
| Total | 590 | 28 | 52 |

**Table D.**

| ITEM | CALORIES | FAT (G) | CARBOHYDRATE (G) |
|---|---|---|---|
| Berry Almond Chicken Salad | 450 | 16 | 43 |
| Nestea Unsweetened Iced Tea | 0 | 0 | 0 |
| Total | 450 | 16 | 43 |

Look, I completely understand. Sometimes nothing else will do. There are just some fundamental needs that a man has to fulfill from time to time. We may have a primal and unrelenting craving for a Big Mac, a Whopper, or the Colonel's Original Recipe. When you have that unwavering need, it is my advice to satisfy it. If you've gotten into the habit of doing the right things, straying from the path a little is not such a bad thing once in a while. As with most of my counsel, however, I'll append my statement with The Single Father's Golden Rule #14: *When you go out to eat, don't order French fries.*

## GOLDEN RULE #14:

*When you go out to eat, don't order French fries.*

Whether you entertain clients or coworkers during the day, whether you spend your days in a cubicle, or whether you work with your hands, the objective is the same. It's important to eat healthy. But it's just as important to be consistent because it's easier to fall into bad habits than it is to create good ones.

If you bring a lunch to work with you, use the same guidelines you use when you make your children's lunches. Use a variety of whole grain breads and lean meats for sandwiches, substitute sliced vegetables for high-fat and high-carbohydrate snacks, add a piece of fruit, and regularly include nuts or yogurt. Occasionally, substitute soup in a thermos for all or part of a sandwich, and exchange either or both for a salad or pasta dish, perhaps left over from the previous night's dinner.

If you have regular access to a cafeteria at work, include a salad with your lunch every day! If your cafeteria is a good one, you'll be able to enjoy one among several choices, which vary by the day. Stay away from fried foods.

Entertaining clients is not all it's cracked up to be and eating out can also become tedious, but there certainly is an upside. For the worker who regularly gets to go to restaurants for lunch and/or dinner, there are almost limitless choices. It's also easier to eat the wrong things or to eat too much. Both can result in feeling sleepy or sluggish after eating because the body is digesting. Eat light, including a lean protein like a chicken breast or fish, a vegetable, and (or just) a salad.

As an aside, consistently eating a healthy lunch from a brown bag, a cafeteria, or a restaurant discretely conveys to coworkers, clients, subordinates, or supervisors that you are a person who "gets it" when it comes to health and fitness. Those people will often make the connection that you also "get it" when it comes to the job, the bottom line, or taking care of your customers. Who knows? Taking care of yourself and your family by eating right and staying fit may have the unintended consequence of career advancement! Even if it doesn't, you'll feel better, you'll be happier because your entire family feels better, and you'll look better, too. That may come in handy.

# EXTRA INNINGS
## THE TIME FOR YOU

It may seem counterintuitive that the section titled "The Time for You" is near the end of *The Single Father's Guide*, especially in light of the fact that I make the point in the Leading Off section reminding you to "Put on your oxygen mask first!" Let me explain.

First of all, what is good for the goslings is good for the gander, and that's a fact. Keeping your commitment to your children, maintaining a balanced diet, creating a healthy lifestyle, and finding ways to stay connected as a family—in short, all the things you've accomplished as a single father—are as good for you as for your children. When you create a healthy meal for your kids, you eat it, too. When you share recreational activities, your children get exercise and relieve stress and so do you. When you find interests in common with your children, you're able to connect with one another so you can help them through the challenges of growing up, and they are able to connect better with you. (Of course, there'll be stages in your children's lives during which you don't really think you're connecting—but your actions will have built a lot of goodwill!)

Second, it clearly follows that if the children aren't happy, then the single father isn't happy either. Imagine if, due in part to an inability to communicate with one of your kids, you are unable to help that child with homework and he or she struggles in school. This, by itself, is a concern. Now, imagine your child gets teased because of these academic struggles or

other things, and bigger problems surface. Under any circumstance, single fatherhood will often be extremely difficult. Can you imagine, though, how difficult it would be for you to relax and enjoy the company of other adults when you know your child is suffering with these problems or something worse?

So, in many ways, maybe in just about all ways, taking care of your family and taking care of yourself is the same thing. Of course, there may be one or two differences.

## Vodka Tonic Highball

1½ ounces vodka

8 ounces sugar-free tonic water

1 cup ice cubes

¼ lime, cut into wedges

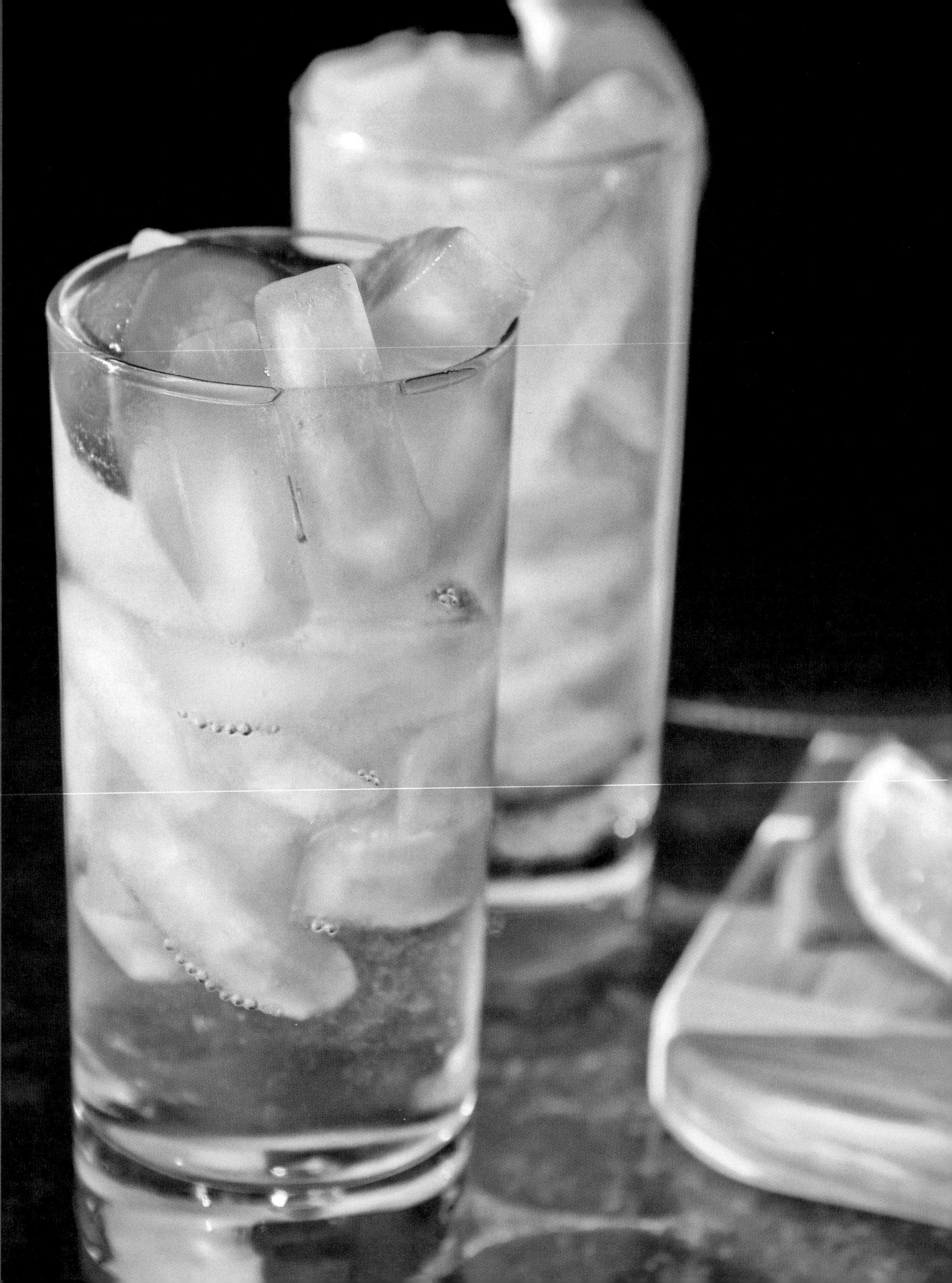

Fill a 16-ounce tumbler with ice. Add vodka, sugar-free tonic water, and a lime wedge. Stir gently, and enjoy after the kids are in bed and you're catching up with the scores on *Baseball Tonight* on ESPN. This one's just for you, Pops.

Look, I don't advocate for or disapprove of responsible alcohol use by persons of legal age. Depending upon one's family or personal experience with alcohol, there may or may not be a stigma associated with it. However, alcohol use is a fact of life in our society, and for a single father who wants to enjoy the occasional cocktail, there is a way to do it.

The U.S. Department of Health and Human Services defines drinking in moderation "as having no more than 1 drink per day for women and no more than 2 drinks per day for men. This definition is referring to the amount consumed on any single day and is not intended as an average over several days."[21]

---

**MODERATE ALCOHOL CONSUMPTION MAY PROVIDE SOME HEALTH BENEFITS. IT MAY:**

- **Reduce your risk of heart disease**
- **Reduce your risk of heart attack**
- **Possibly reduce your risk of strokes, particularly ischemic strokes**
- **Lower your risk of gallstones**
- **Possibly reduce your risk of diabetes**[22]

---

I'm sure scientific studies have been conducted to reach these conclusions and that research balances the negative impact of alcohol on internal organs, like the liver, with benefits of the relaxation, reduction of stress, and social interaction that often accompanies alcohol consumption. Obviously, overuse can result in addiction, which is in direct opposition to the Golden Rule #5: *There is no wrong way to grieve, as long as you don't hurt anyone in the process.*

Alcoholism is a thief that steals your time, your money, your health, and your motivation. The waste of those invaluable resources is not only a detriment to you, but also adversely affects your children by shifting your attention from the welfare of your family to consuming alcohol and recovering after overconsumption.

Another concern related to consuming alcoholic beverages is the additional empty calories alcohol adds to your diet. The average premium beer contains about 150 calories, and having a couple of beers is the equivalent of almost 15 percent of your daily RDA for calories. A five-ounce glass of wine or one and a half ounces of liquor are comparable in calories, but add a sugary mixer to the liquor, and the empty calories skyrocket!

(As an aside, to burn the additional calories from the consumption of two alcoholic beverages, the average man would have to perform twenty to thirty minutes of high-intensity aerobic exercise!)

If everything at your disposal is a tool you can use to improve your quality of life, then choose your tools wisely and use each one to your benefit. In my humble opinion, the benefits of having the occasional cocktail or two outweighs the disadvantages of the additional calories. The "medicinal" benefits from consuming an adult beverage once in a while, for example, as a stress reliever or a nonprescription sleep aid, is preferable to a prescription and much less expensive.

Bear in mind, alcohol is a diuretic. Personally, I prefer a glass of wine or a cocktail to beer, which contains more liquid, because I'm more likely to sleep without the unrelenting need for bladder relief at 4:00 a.m. If you prefer a cocktail, refer to the Single Father's Golden Rule #13 and use a sugar-free mixer.

In his 2007 novel *Playing for Pizza*, John Grisham narrates a story in which a fictional, disgraced former NFL quarterback, Rick Dockery, moves to Italy and plays football for a semipro (American) football team in exchange for the metaphorical equivalent of pizza. Grisham describes a photograph of Rick's aging teammate, Tommaso, who had been thirty pounds heavier earlier in his career: "He looked huge, and Rick almost said some of that bulk would be welcome now . . . No doubt losing the extra weight had much to do with his love life.[23]" If art imitates life, then Grisham may be on to something.

Depending on your circumstance and, in the case of the divorced or widowed father, depending on how you've chosen to grieve, you may at some point want to pursue a romantic interest. As men, we enjoy spending time with a partner who is emotionally and physically attractive, and many potential partners will appreciate the same qualities in a man. While a potential long-term relationship may be based more on personal traits like character, integrity, compassion, or spontaneity, the initial attraction between two people is almost always based on physical characteristics.

A single father who adopts a healthy lifestyle for himself and for his children will soon discover he is leaner, healthier, and more confident. An unintended consequence of this lifestyle is that the single dad will also demonstrate that he is not only a good provider for his family, but also an accomplished caregiver for his dependent children. Potential romantic partners may just find that combination appealing.

As previously noted, others may have expectations relating to how you should and should not behave under a variety of conditions, including dating. However, it's not your responsibility to take care of anyone other than yourself and your children. When it comes to whether to date and when, make your own decision.

As far as I'm concerned, there is no "rule" for when a single father can start to date. Obviously, you have emotional, intellectual, and physical needs. You are built with the desire to fulfill those needs. On the flipside, you are equipped to satisfy another person's needs, as well. Frankly, you have a lot to offer.

*I don't know why people*
*like the home run*
*so much. A home run is over as soon*
*as it starts. . . . The triple is the most*
*exciting play of the game.*
*A triple is like meeting a woman who*
*excites you, spending the evening*
*talking and getting more excited,*
*then taking her home. It drags on and on.*
*You're never sure how it's*
*going to turn out.*
—George Foster

You'll have dates. If it's been a while since you've dated, and if you're anything like I was, you'll find the contemporary dating scene very different from when you were last an active participant. That's okay. Approach it as an adventure and a learning process. You'll meet people whose company you enjoy and others who you'll quickly determine you don't enjoy. The range of emotions experienced by the women you'll date will be similar to what you experience.

While it may be easier said than done, don't worry too much if you don't immediately find "chemistry."

Likely, you will eventually meet someone with whom you want to spend more time and who will want to spend more time with you. The two of you enjoy the other's company, and you learn you're a better man, a better father for the time you spend with your romantic interest. You may discover that you want to spend more time with that person, and, if you have full custody, you start to hire a sitter for your kids once or twice a week. If you share custody, then dating is a little less of a logistical challenge, but in any case, there will come a time when you discover the "balance" in your life begins to tilt away from center. It's at this point when single fatherhood is more an art than a science.

When I've dated, I haven't introduced my children to my romantic interests any time during the first several encounters to avoid creating unrealistic expectations or misunderstandings for just about everyone. In my case, if my children met a woman for whom I have a romantic interest, they might wonder or even hope the woman would become their "new mom." At the same time, my romantic interest upon meeting my children may get an impression that I *only* want to find a mother for my children and get spooked, or prematurely begin to envision herself in that role.

When the balance of the responsibilities I have as a parent and those I have to a romantic partner begin to tilt, however, I have to consider new variables. At the point when I want to spend more time with a woman I'm dating, I clearly have an interest in the person beyond a casual friendship. If my partner feels the same way, together we want to explore the potential of the relationship in a more meaningful way. To do this, I'd need to invest at least the same amount of time, if not more, with that person, but the balance has already shifted. The relationship would have reached the level of emotional intimacy by this time that my partner would no longer be spooked by or have unrealistic expectations for our relationship; however, nothing would have necessarily changed from my children's perspectives. It is at this point where I consider the benefits and detriments of commingling my personal life with my home life, considering my needs and those of my children first.

To deny the relationship an opportunity to grow and perhaps become something more, I believe, is unfair to me. But to give the relationship that opportunity, my partner and I need to spend more time together. To spend more time together, I'd have to either reduce the time I spend with my

## GOLDEN RULE #15:

*It should be an exception that you introduce your children to your romantic interest, and do so only if you are reasonably certain there is potential for a relatively long-term relationship.*

children or involve my romantic interest in family activities. If I decrease the quality time with my children, I further reduce the parenting my children receive. If I involve the person I'm dating with my family, I risk creating the hope for my children of a "whole," two-parent family, which could end in disappointment.

To resolve this dilemma, I have never introduced my children to a first date. For any early outings with a new person or, in cases that the kids happen to already know the person with whom I plan to go out, I don't even tell the kids I have a date. If after several dates usually spanning a few weeks or months, however, I've developed a degree of intimacy with my partner and I am certain beyond any reasonable doubt that she has my best interests and those of my kids at heart, I will introduce my partner to my children and begin to involve her in family activities. During those times, I'm able to see another side of the person who is clearly now my "girlfriend," while my girlfriend and I continue to explore interests and compatibility. Naturally, then, The Single Father's Golden Rule #15 is *It should be an exception that you introduce your children to your romantic interest, and do so only if you are reasonably certain there is potential for a relatively long-term relationship.*

I have introduced my children to women I've dated. I've made a mistake or two, which illustrates my contention that this decision is often more an art than a science. After spending time, openly communicating, and experiencing the ways another person reacts to various situations, you often can get a good idea of that person's character. If, after you've made the decision to introduce your romantic interest to your children, you discover a previously hidden quality that is contrary to your value system or you eventually realize for practical reasons that the prospect for a long-term commitment is unlikely, it's better to address the situation sooner rather than later. Have a calm, reasoned, and honest conversation. If the person really is who you thought she was when you introduced her to your children, she'll continue to be a friend to you and to

*Things could be worse. Suppose your errors were counted and published every day, like those of a baseball player.*
—**Author unknown**

your family. In that case, your children will learn the valuable life lesson that the nature of relationships may change over time, but friendships can endure.

# Third-Date Fruity Nutty Salad
# with Sautéed Vegetable Lamb Chops

1 head iceberg lettuce

2 sliced carrots

1 sliced tomato

½ sliced cucumber

½ cup sliced mushrooms

¼ cup dried cranberries

¼ cup raw cashews

¼ cup shredded cheddar cheese

2 lamb chops

1 sliced green pepper

1 sliced yellow pepper

1 sliced onion

2 cloves garlic, crushed

1 tablespoon olive oil

½ teaspoon salt

¼ teaspoon pepper

For the salad, remove the outer leaf and core from the lettuce, hand shred in a colander, and rinse. Toss with carrots, cucumber, mushrooms, cranberries, cashews, and shredded cheese. Dress with your favorite vinaigrette.

To cook the lamb chops and vegetables, heat a large frying pan to medium or medium-high. Add the olive oil, lamb chops, peppers, onion, garlic, salt, and pepper. While regularly stirring the vegetables, cook the lamb 4 to 8 minutes on each side, depending on how rare or well-done you prefer the meat. Enjoy with a bottle of wine with an interesting adult when there's no one else in the house.

While this is a tasty and a fairly simple meal to create, it offers very interesting fringe benefits for you and your date. First, considering the variety of ingredients required, this is a great "punctuation meal." Simply put, it's the perfect end to a perfect day-long date, which, at some point, would have included shopping for all kinds of fresh vegetables together. There's just something about shopping at an open-air farmer's market, where a couple can talk, laugh, and handle fresh produce that promotes emotional intimacy. Next, while the recipe is not complicated, it does require active preparation. The tearing, slicing, tossing, crushing, turning, and stirring need doing, and of course, you do it together. While you tear, your partner stirs. While your partner is crushing, you're turning. Who knows? If you trust one another with knives, you can do the slicing together. Finally, when the work is finished, the two of you have created a wonderful meal that has a pleasantly colorful presentation.

More importantly, you've shared an experience, accomplished something tangible, and created a rapport that has a rather immediate gratification! The two of you get to eat the food you bought, prepared, and cooked together. All the time, you've communicated and enjoyed one another's company.

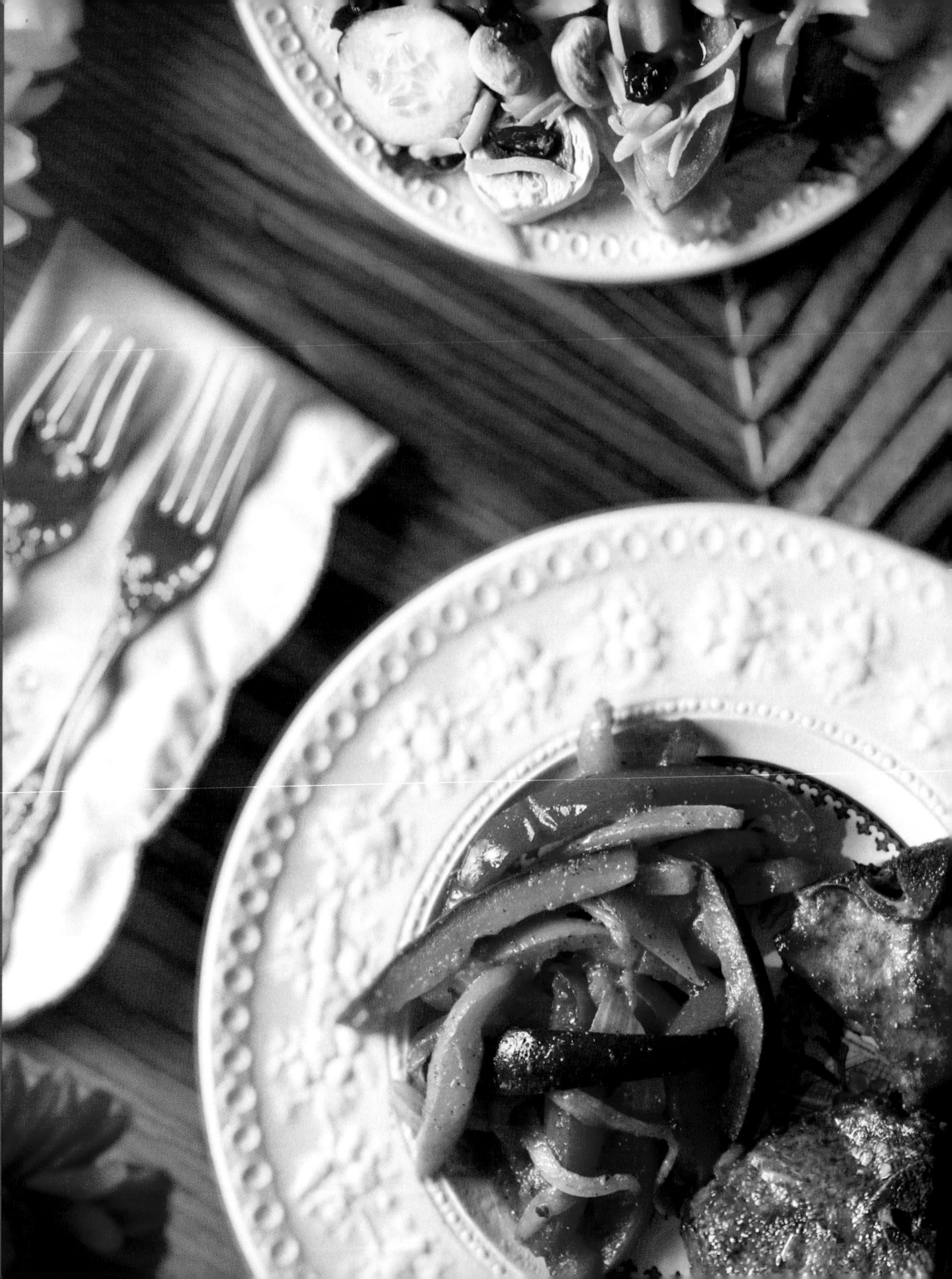

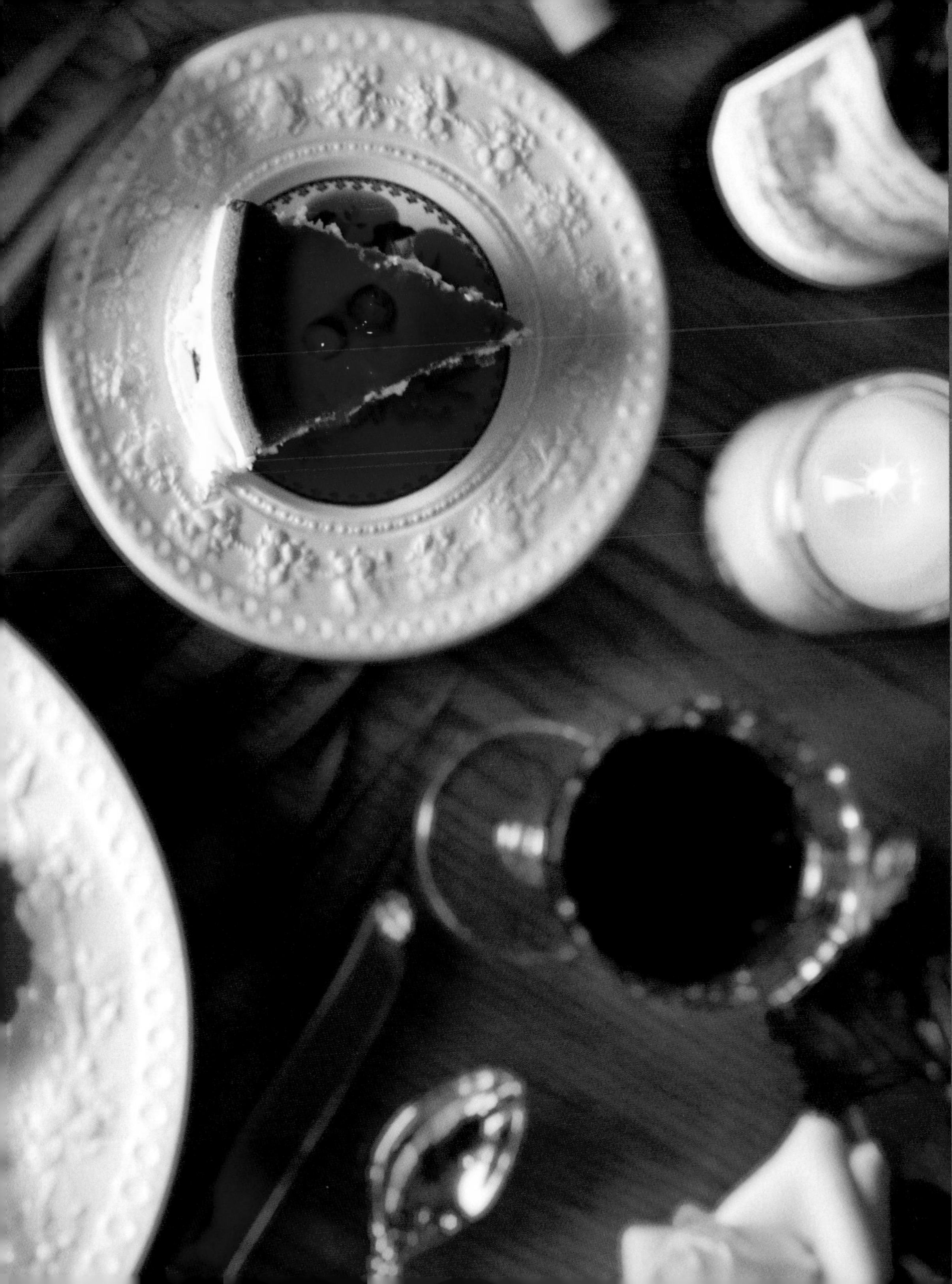

# Frozen Strawberry Margaritas

16 ounces water

1 packet sugar-free lemonade drink
   mix

6 ounces tequila

2 ounces triple sec

12 ounces frozen strawberries

1 lime, peeled

1 orange, peeled

Course salt (optional)

Ice (optional)

To make the sour mix, add 16 ounces of water with 1 packet of sugar-free lemonade drink mix. (The drink mix is intended to make 2 quarts of lemonade, but the packet concentrated in the pint of water makes a very good, calorie-free sour mix.) Add sour mix, tequila, triple sec, strawberries, lime, and orange to blender. Puree. Add additional ice for more "frozen" consistency, if desired. Serve with course salt on the rim of glass. Makes four cool cocktails—that's two for you and two for a friend, if you're keeping score at home.

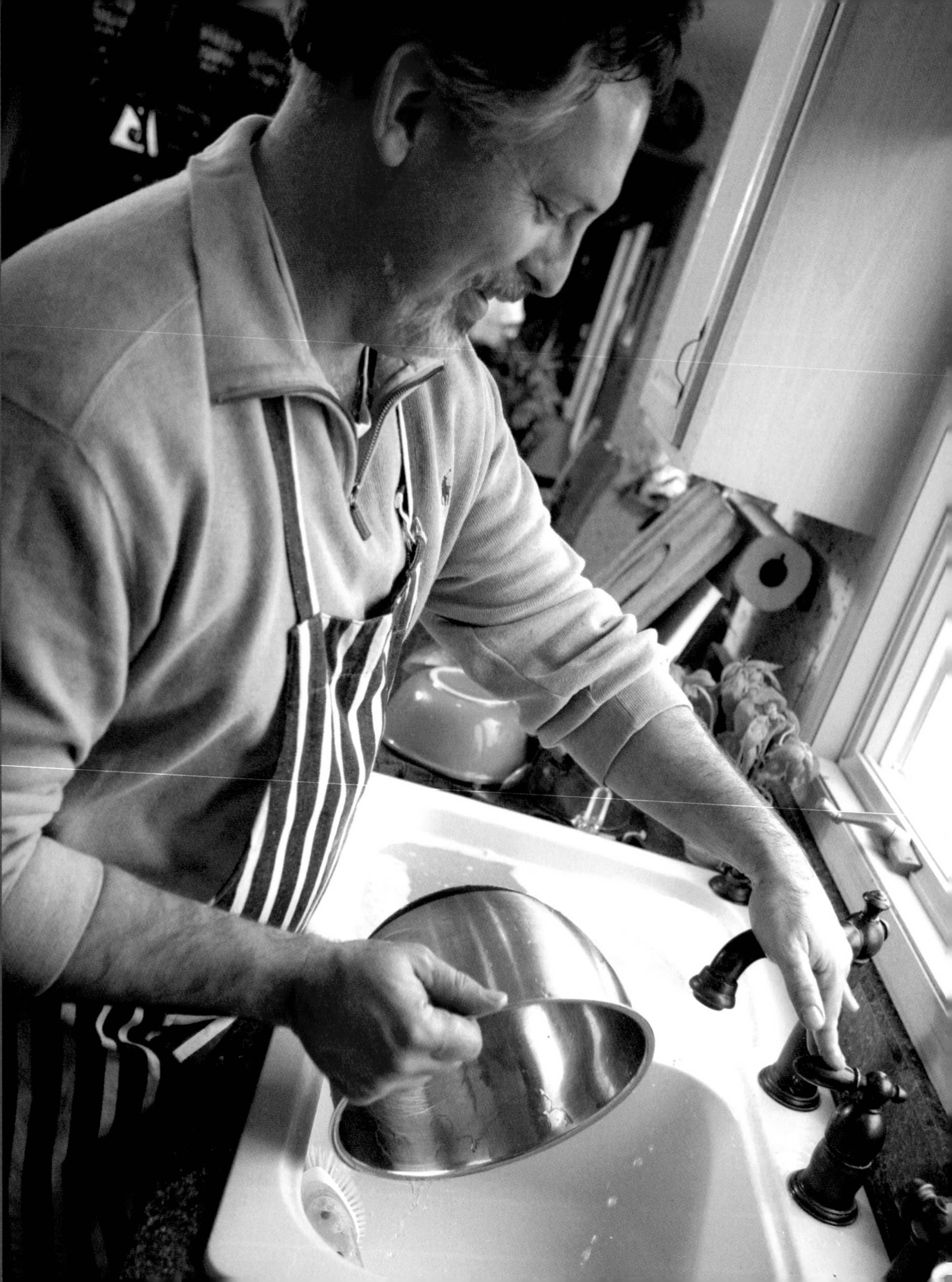

# POSTGAME
## THE SINGLE FATHER'S GOLDEN RULES

Every few months, it seems, I get a phone call. Well, I get a few more phone calls, but the phone call I get every few months is the same call. The only difference is the person who dialed my number. Before I answer, I'm usually able to identify the caller as a PFF by checking the Caller ID. Based on the nature of the friendship and the length of time that elapsed since my last conversation with the caller, I am often able to predict the reason for the call even before I answer the phone. It often goes something like this:

**PFF:** Hey! How are you?

**ME:** Things are pretty good, thanks. My life is crazy, but the kids are healthy and so am I. Can't complain . . . much! How 'bout you?

**PFF:** I'm good. And, well, you know, it's been a while since we've spoken, and I'm not sure whether you'd be comfortable talking about this, but I have a friend, _____, who (a) recently divorced, or (b) lost his wife. He has _____ small children.

**ME:** I'm very sorry, PFF.

**PFF:** Yeah, me too. He's a great guy, and well, he's sort of overwhelmed. And, I couldn't help but notice that you seem to be doing okay with all of your stuff.

**ME:** Thanks, PFF. I think I have pretty good idea how he feels.

**PFF:** Yeah. That's sort of the reason I called. I wonder if you wouldn't mind talking with him. I thought maybe you can give him some advice or some ideas, you know, to cope with everything . . .

Of course, there are a lot more divorced men who are single fathers than there are men who've lost their wives. Regardless, among the calls I've received from well-intentioned PFF's, I've yet to get one call directly from a newly minted single father.

There are a lot of reasons for the reluctance of a recently divorced or widowed dad to call some guy he doesn't know to talk about the failure of his marriage, the loss of his partner, or his inability to cope with raising his children. (Would there have to be any other reasons?) Most guys just don't like to communicate on that level with other people, much less with a stranger who is a friend of woman he knows and about whom the woman describes as seeming "to be doing okay." (Huh? I wonder why none of these guys called!) Heck. I was reluctant to talk with anyone about my situation, too, and I consider myself to be a better-than-average communicator and fairly open in terms of my emotional perspectives.

I was fortunate, though. I got great advice from family and friends who were confident enough in their friendship and relationship with me to say "Hey! I've been through this. Listen!" I also acquired, reluctantly at times, a set of skills that helped me deal with the challenges of single parenthood. Then what I didn't know, I learned as I went. As long as my intentions were pure, I've never been afraid of making mistakes.

If any of those new single fathers about whom one of my PFFs solicited my help had called, I would have suggested two or three of what I considered the most important among The Single Father's Golden Rules. Attempting to discuss all fifteen would be too time-consuming. Frankly, some are minor-league level, while others are hall-of-fame caliber. Sometimes, less is more.

Fortunately, with *The Single Father's Guide*, I'm not restricted by time, so the reader has the luxury to refer to the theory as he practices.

Which among The Single Father's Golden Rules are most important? Well, I think they're all important, but every single father has his own set of strengths and weaknesses. What's most important to one man will be less important to another. In my opinion, though, a hitter has to get on base before he can score a run.

Still, if that call ever did come from that guy to whom my PFF gave my phone number, I'd tell him, "Put on your oxygen mask first. In the

*Love is the most important thing in the world, but baseball is pretty good too.*
**—Author unknown**

face of what could potentially be an overwhelming change to your family, maintain your routines and traditions. And, there is no wrong way to grieve as long as you don't hurt anyone in the process."

Good luck, single father. Your effort is worthwhile in ways you cannot fathom.

# THE SINGLE FATHER'S GOLDEN RULES:

**GOLDEN RULE #1:**
*Put on your oxygen mask first!*

**GOLDEN RULE #2:**
*Include at least one vegetable or fruit with every meal.*

**GOLDEN RULE #3:**
*Maintain your routines and traditions.*

**GOLDEN RULE #4:**
*Take a fiber supplement along with your vitamins with at least eight ounces of liquid every morning during breakfast.*

**GOLDEN RULE #5:**
*There is no wrong way to grieve as long as you don't hurt anyone in the process.*

**GOLDEN RULE #6:**
*Dad is NOT a short-order cook!*

**GOLDEN RULE #7:**
*Make friends with mothers of your children's friends, and then be a friend . . . a platonic friend.*

**GOLDEN RULE #8:**
*If you don't bring junk food home in your grocery bags, you and your children won't eat it!*

**GOLDEN RULE #9:**
*Anyone can take from the snack bowl any time!*

### GOLDEN RULE #10:
*No television on weekdays.*

#### COROLLARY:
*Electronic devices may be used only on the first floor . . . and not in bedrooms.*

### GOLDEN RULE #11:
*Identify at least one activity that your family enjoys and is one in which you can regularly participate together.*

### GOLDEN RULE #12:
*If you already have a family pet when you become a single father, keep it. If you don't already have a family pet when you become a single father, for the sake of your sanity, don't get one!*

### GOLDEN RULE #13:
*Replace sugary drinks, including soft drinks, fruit juices, and energy drinks with water or other no-sugar-added beverages.*

### GOLDEN RULE #14:
*When you go out to eat, don't order French fries.*

### GOLDEN RULE #15:
*It should be an exception that you introduce your children to your romantic interest, and do so only if you are reasonably certain there is potential for a relatively long-term relationship.*

# ACKNOWLEDGMENTS

In yet another example of baseball as analogy for life, Robert De Niro's character, Al Capone, in the film *The Untouchables*, gives a "motivational" speech to his lieutenants:

"A man stands alone at home plate. This is a time for what? For individual achievement. Then, he stands alone. But, in the field, what? Part of a team. Looks, throws, catches, hustles. Part of one big team. Bats, himself, the live long day . . . if his team doesn't field, what is he?"[24]

> *Only in baseball can a team player be a pure individualist first and a team player second, within the rules and spirit of the game.*
> —**Branch Rickey**

While the tone and mood of that scene in *The Untouchables* are quite different from those in *The Single Father's Guide*, the analogy is a good one. Creating this recipe for single fatherhood is an example of my turn at bat, but this project would have been quite a bit more difficult to complete without the support, encouragement, and friendship of quite a few people.

First, thanks to my parents, Lucy and Tom. Mom, while I resisted the babysitting classes you insisted that I take when I was a ten-year-old boy, I'm glad that you found a way to get me there. Like a lot of things, I couldn't have realized how much those seeds would grow into indispensible skills as I've matured into an adult. Dad, thanks for introducing me to baseball, basketball, and football, and then encouraging my love and understanding of those and other sports throughout childhood and adulthood. To my

Uncle Jim, I appreciated the opportunity as a young man to have worked for you at Mattingly's Sports Bar & Grill in Florissant, Missouri, first as a janitor, then a busboy (yes), a short-order cook, and eventually, a bartender. You gave me the chance to learn the restaurant business from a guy who knows the business and knows people. At some point, I'd really appreciate getting your recipe for Mattingly's award-winning Cajun Wings. I promise I won't publish it!

The playgroup in which my son participated almost every week from the time he was eighteen months old until he was five years old was the place I learned a lot about the nuances of parenting from some great people and PFFs. Those great ladies include Lisa Conklin, Laurie Germain, Kim McGowan, Jen Ruffo, and Annette Silva. In addition, "Aunt" Phyllis Kaminsky and Trish Miller not only were a couple of the best neighbors a guy could have, but also provided a great deal of their time and counsel during the early days of my single fatherhood. As I'd previously mentioned, Steve White had the confidence and foresight to get my attention and to give me a critical bit of perspective during a time when I most needed it, even though I didn't know it at the time.

Old and new friends who served as intrepid readers of the first draft of *The Single Father's Guide* include grief counselor Kandy Magnotti; Dan Lambrecht; Kim Sumner-Mayer, PhD, LMFT, who also provided great insights that added dimension to some of my observations and ideas; and, finally, Karen LoSchiavo, PsyD, who has been both an insightful playgroup mom and a great PFF. Thank you for your time, comments, constructively critical reviews, and encouragement.

Sharon Scott was another manuscript reader who provided not only feedback but an unexpected benefit as well. In addition to being an accomplished author and one of my de facto mentors during the past few years, Sharon is the one of the founders of Arundel Publishing. After completing her reading of the draft, Sharon made some great suggestions and then asked me to become an "Arundel Author." I am fortunate to be a part of the team.

It turned out that I had met Kathie McLachlan Austin when she bought a copy of my first title, *Father Like A Tree*, at a children's book festival in 2005. Five years later, the two of us hadn't realized we'd already met when she and I bumped into one another again at a local café. It was a fortuitous meeting. Since then, Kathie has become a close friend, confidante, muse, and sounding board for a variety of parenting and creative issues. In addition, Kathie was the first to read an early version of *The Single Father's Guide*, provided comments and encouragement during the entire process, and continues to be "my kind of crazy."

Finally, although "thanks" doesn't seem to be quite the right word, my children, Jordan, Katie, and Wade, have given me a singular purpose. I'm incredibly proud of you for growing up to be strong, beautiful, and intelligent people, and I'm lucky to be the man you call "Dad."

# NOTES

1 Earl Kelly, "Single Dads Give, Learn Valuable Lessons," *Capital Gazette*, June 19, 2011.

2 "Facts for Features," U.S. Census Bureau, www.census.gov, April 20, 2011.

3 Ron Shelton, *Bull Durham*, The Mount Company, June 15, 1988.

4 Sabrina Stapleton, "RDA Calories Per Day," Livestrong.com, March 28, 2011.

5 "Childhood Obesity," National Center for Chronic Disease Prevention and Health Promotion, Division of Adolescent and School Health, www.cdc.gov, October 20, 2008.

6 Gale Sayers, *I Am Third* (New York: Viking Press, 1970).

7 Interview with Kim Sumner-Mayer, PhD, LMFT, December 6, 2011.

8 Food Database and Calorie Counter: Whole Wheat Flour, White Flour, FatSecret.com.

9 Food Database and Calorie Counter : ⅓ Cup Soy Flour, FatSecret.com.

10 Food Database and Calorie Counter : ⅓ Cup White Flour, FatSecret.com.

11 Food Database and Calorie Counter : ½ Cup Granulated Sugar, FatSecret.com.

12 Interview with Kim Sumner-Mayer, PhD, LMFT, December 6, 2011.

13 "Grief," National Center for Biotechnology Information, U.S. National Library of Medicine, www.ncbi.nlm.nih.gov, 2011.

14 Nancy Shute, "Americans Are Fat, and Expected to Get Much Fatter," www.npr.org, November 17, 2011.

15 "McDonald's USA Nutrition Facts for Popular Menu Items," McDonald's USA, January 2007.

16 *Children's Diets in the Mid-1990's: Dietary Intake and Its Relationship with School Meal Participation*. Mathematica Policy Research, Inc. Final report submitted to the U.S. Department of Agriculture, January 2001.

17 "Is There a Reason He Won't Ask for Directions?" *Edmonton Journal*, June 4, 2008.

18 Arthur Agatston, MD, "How America Got So Fat (and So Sick)," *Prevention*, October 2011, pp. 100–107.

19 "The Road to Hell Is Paved with Good Intentions," Wikipedia.com, May 26, 2011.

20 "Nutritional Facts," Wendys.com, 2011

21 "Alcoholic Beverages," in *Dietary Guidelines for Americans* (Washington, DC: U.S. Government Printing Office), 2005, pp. 43–46. http://www.health.gov/DIETARYGUIDELINES/dga2005/document/html/chapter9.htm. Accessed March 28, 2008.

22 "Alcohol Use: If You Drink, Keep It Moderate," www.MayoClinic.com, Mayo Foundation for Medical Education and Research (MFMER), March 15, 2011.

23 John Grisham, *Playing for Pizza* (New York: Doubleday, 2007) p. 225.

24 Oscar Fraley, Eliot Ness, and David Mamet, *The Untouchables*, 1987.